S0-BAG-796

SEXUAL ANARCHY

DAVE MILLER, PH. D.

APOLOGETICS PRESS

Apologetics Press, Inc.
230 Landmark Drive
Montgomery, Alabama 36117-2752

© Copyright 2006
ISBN-10: 0-932859-81-X
ISBN-13: 978-932859-81-5

Printed in China

All rights reserved. No part of this book may be reproduced in any form without permission from the publisher, except in the case of brief quotations embodied in articles or critical reviews.

Library of Congress Cataloging-in-Publication
Dave Miller (1953 -)
Sexual Anarchy
Includes bibliographic references.
ISBN-10: 0-932859-81-X
ISBN-13: 978-932859-81-5
1. Ethics of family relationships 2. Christian experience, practice & life 3. Philosophy and theory of religion 4. Christianity and other belief systems 5. Social interactions 6. Factors affecting social behavior 7. Culture & institutions I. Title

241–dc22   2005909988

DEDICATION

To Deb–
whose positive influence on my life
has been inestimable, profound,
and eternal

TABLE OF CONTENTS

PREFACE

The *American Heritage Dictionary* gives three definitions for "anarchy": (1) Absence of any form of political authority; (2) political disorder and confusion; and (3) absence of any cohesive principle, such as a common standard or purpose (2000, p. 65). This book addresses itself to the sexual anarchy that characterizes America. Since the 1960s, American civilization has been sucked into the vortex of sexual disorder and confusion. The sexual behavior of many Americans is determined on the basis of personal choice—what feels good. More specifically, the mind has been disengaged and fleshly passions and bodily appetites have been allowed to inform the mind what actions may be taken. "Barnyard morality" is the order of the day. Though humans did not evolve from animals, but were, in fact, created in the image of their Creator (Genesis 1:26-27; cf. Lyons and Thompson, 2002), when the human spirit (the mind) is disengaged from the objective standard of morality, humans become animalistic—behaving like brute beasts.

The dismantling of the Christian foundations of America during the last fifty years has resulted in a plethora of sexually deviant actions. America is literally spiraling downward into the abyss of moral depravity and degradation. While sex is inherently good, having been created by the Creator Who fashioned the male and female bodies, it is only good when it is practiced in accordance with the stipulations framed by the Creator. Deviation from that moral framework inevitably wreaks psychological, emotional, spiritual, and physical havoc on the individuals involved, and on society at large.

Sexual anarchy is taking place on many fronts. The massive assault on sexual morals commenced with the "New Morality" in the turbulent 1960s, when American culture began a foundational realigning and transformation in values, beliefs, and norms

(Chapter 1). By 1965, the divorce rate literally exploded—a trend that continues to this day with little abatement—inflicting inexorable damage to large numbers of children, shaking the very foundations of society, and destroying its underpinnings: the home and family (Chapter 2). As sexual mores were jettisoned, couples who did not enact multiple marriages simply "lived together" and moved from one sexual partner to another. The children who were conceived by these self-indulgent, sexual escapades were unwanted, evoking the deafening clamor for the legalization of abortion. They got their wish, when the Supreme Court gave them an unholy nod in 1973 (Chapter 3). The systematic implementation of the radical Feminist agenda was well underway, with the push for passage of the ERA, which included redefining gender roles and the traditional American family, as well as the celebration of lesbian relationships. The sinister campaign to achieve normalcy was executed with unflinching determination to bully the American public into first tolerating, then accepting, and finally legalizing homosexuality (Chapter 4). In the early 1970s, every major mental health organization in the country quickly fell into step with the party line. Concomitant with this progressive deterioration of sexual mores has been the pernicious encroachment of pornography (Chapter 5).

Every one of these social factors—divorce, abortion, homosexuality, and pornography—share in common the fact that they are all linked to human sexuality. They all represent human desire to gratify sexual appetites without regard to a higher standard of authority. But no civilization, no nation, no country can survive the ultimate affects of sexual anarchy. Many in America appear determined to pursue the same road to perdition that every previous civilization followed. If a sizable percentage of this country's citizenry persists in doing so, mark it down, America, too, will eventually collapse into the dust of antiquity—like every other civilization in human history.

CHAPTER ONE

SEX AND THE SIXTIES

American civilization had managed to survive the devastating and catastrophic effects of economic depression and world war. Anticipating a bright and prosperous future, the "Greatest Generation" attacked their environment with unleashed optimism and settled into a way of life that has become the envy of the civilized world. American society began the process of realigning and readjusting itself to cope with a new phase of social evolution. The postwar era brought technological and material prosperity.

Into this cultural matrix came the generation of the fifties and sixties–those of us known as "baby boomers"–the postwar product of parents who had been tried and refined in the fires of suffering and hardship. Anxious to give us the comforts of which they had been deprived during the 1930s and 1940s, but for which the blood of many Americans had been sacrificed, our parents provided us with a pleasant existence. Religious interests were integrated into this comfortable lifestyle, but these were largely reserved for, and confined to, Sunday. Nevertheless, American society in general remained linked with, and committed, to certain clear-cut foundational principles. These values included a common recognition of what is right and wrong, that God had blessed America and seen her through trying times, and that America had been blessed with freedom–not freedom **from** religion, but freedom **for** religion: the **Christian** religion.

The World War II generation was, in many ways, the climax and pinnacle of the moral, spiritual, and religious excellence latent in the original intentions of the Founding Fathers of America. They were the embodiment of their parents' belief system that typified American greatness. Tragically, social circumstances prevented this truly American framework from being transferred to the next generation.

THE BABY BOOMERS IN THE 1960s

To say that something happened in the 1960s would be an understatement. The uncontrolled nature of rock and roll music, motorcycle gangs, and the beatniks that appeared in the '50s were undoubtedly harbingers of the chaos that was to characterize the '60s. In music, the Beach Boys and the Beatles were contemporaneous manifestations of the largely innocent and clean-cut being replaced by new directions and new definitions. Then came Vietnam, the hippies, drugs, and the "generation gap." We found ourselves growing up in a societal environment, a social milieu that was suddenly being assaulted by staggering complexities of existence. We were bombarded with a whole new set of rules for playing the game of life. A new world view and a new set of explanations for the meaning of our existence were introduced.

The answers given to our questions about life's meaning amounted to the notion that there really were no absolute answers. The simple life of our predecessors was being challenged, in light of the complexities associated with "modern" living. With no firm answers, fewer and fewer certainties, and few rules remaining intact for coping with life, we were left to flounder amid increasingly firm and adamant declarations that such floundering was, in fact, the true answer to life's perplexities. The only certainty was that there was no certainty! Ethical and moral relativism was gradually embedding itself into our consciousness. We were badgered to "keep an open mind" and refrain from being "judgmental." Consequently, our convictions were neutralized, and we were made to retreat from making moral distinctions.

As small children, we were terrorized with the prospects of nuclear disaster as we cowered under our metal school desks, heads down and hands clasped over the back of our necks—practicing, drilling for the possibility of nuclear holocaust. We were made to realize the tenuous, shaky uncertainties of even our own political system when we saw on national television blood from our President's head splattered all over the dress of a grieving wife. We experienced cataclysmic cultural progress within just a few short years: from props to jets, from sputniks to men on the Moon, from eight millimeter film to video tape, from mimeograph to Xerox, from the atomic bomb to nuclear missiles and star wars, from polio vaccine to organ transplants.

We were made to feel that we were not responsible—for life's mess, the world's mess, and the mess our own lives were gradually becoming. As society deteriorated before our eyes, psychologists told us that the way our parents treated us as children made us who we were, and that there was no point trying to change and be someone we were not. We were told to just "be ourselves," which meant we were free to "do our own thing" and not feel guilty about it. Our schoolteachers told us that the old ways of teaching (which consisted of lecture and information transfer) and the old ideas being taught (absolutes of right and wrong, views of God and morality) were traditional, outdated, and ineffective. We were faced with a "brave new world." We were introduced to new methods of teaching that centered on group consensus and "individual tastes." We no longer were required to meet the demands of a lecturer who expected us to absorb and master a specific amount of information. Now we could work at our own pace and be free to push ourselves at whatever rate we were capable of or felt comfortable with—which wasn't much. We were told by our science teachers that, oh, we could still believe in the Bible if we chose to—but that it just didn't happen the way the Bible said it did. Humans are merely the result of evolution.

An orchestra of voices—from *Ramparts* magazine, Timothy Leary, the Beatles, and Peter and Jane Fonda to Ravi Shankar and the Maharishi Mahesh Yogi—goaded us to recognize the legitimate, even preferable, alternatives to the American value system. We were encouraged by Janis Joplin, Jimi Hendrix, Steppenwolf, Jefferson Airplane, Canned Heat, Iron Butterfly, Cream, Deep Purple, Frank Zappa, and a host of other groups to materialize our frustration by turning on and dropping out. We grew to hate war, the draft board, the establishment, the government, our parents, their religion, and their country. We tried to return to nature with communes and trips to the backwoods and Colorado. Nudity, "free love," co-ed dorms, long hair, incense, water pipes, hashish, acid, grass, speed, Roman sandals, headbands, beads, peace symbols, roach clips, "granny" glasses, panel trucks, sitars, and concerts with light shows were some of the facets of our lifestyle that helped to numb our dissatisfaction with reality.

MITIGATING SOCIAL FACTORS

The value system that punctuates this social scenario was undergirded by several pervasive social factors. First, the mainstream baby-boomer generation is in large part **a rebellious generation that rejects authority**. Looking back to the 1960s, one is surely struck by the fact that rebellion was a central feature of what took place. The younger generation and the older generation clashed sharply, creating "the generation gap." Remember the saying: "Don't trust anyone over thirty"? (Notice that we baby boomers have dropped that cliché!). The younger generation was, in reality, rebelling against the older generation by challenging and rejecting the values and principles that characterized the preceding generation. The cultural turmoil that was manifested in the 1960s in the form of long hair, antiwar, anti-Establishment, use of drugs, acceptance of Eastern religion, etc., was nothing other than a rebellion against authority. The rebellious younger generation behaved in precisely the same fashion as any over-indulged, spoiled child behaves. Lacking the discipline he so desperately needs to inculcate self-control and personal restraint, he clamors for his own way—even though he is uncertain from moment to moment as to what that way is.

The fruit of the '60s decade of rebellion against authority is now evident: a full-scale breakdown in respect for authority. Since 1965, crime rates have literally skyrocketed. America has more crime and more criminals than ever before. By definition, criminals are people who refuse to submit to the authority of the legal system. The American judicial system is clogged and overflowing with cases. Prisons are full, and additional ones cannot be constructed fast enough to keep up with the demand—resulting in early release for dangerous criminal elements. The self-indulgent, "me first" mentality of the "rebel" attitude has led to the widespread, commonplace practice of suing others. You can even sue a fast-food restaurant if you spill their hot coffee on yourself—and win the case!

The lack of respect for authority is seen in the fact that many lawyers are no longer interested in ascertaining guilt or innocence and seeing that justice is served. Now, the objective is to beat the system, look for technicalities to short-circuit the process, and do whatever is necessary to acquit the guilty. We have made a complete mockery of justice, and respectful submission to the laws of the land is a laughing stock. The wise man of antiquity had something to say about just such a scenario: "Because the sentence against an evil work is not executed speedily, therefore the heart of the sons of men is fully set in them to do evil" (Ecclesiastes 8:11). Policemen were once held up as paragons of virtue who commanded respect in society. No decent, upstanding individual in America would dare to have an encounter with a police officer. Such would have been disgraceful. The average American was inevitably a "law-abiding citizen." But now, the authority of the police is openly challenged and undermined. They were called "pigs" and "fuzz" in the 1960s. Now it is even worse. Citizens resist them, cuss them, and even kill them.

The rebellion against authority has been transferred to succeeding generations. Children no longer are being taught to respect and submit to authority. Consequently, gangs are on the increase. Parents are fading into irrelevance and cannot control their own children. Public schools are out of control with children shooting one another and inflicting violence against their teachers. Teachers are leaving their profession, or retiring early, because time ordinarily spent teaching is spent simply trying to maintain control in the classroom. The widespread refusal to submit to authority has essentially become a cultural norm. The restless inclination to have one's own way—this incessant inclination to rebel—is directly related to the sexual anarchy that now prevails.

Second, the baby-boomer generation is very **materialistic**. Baby boomers grew up in a nation that had achieved a higher standard of living, and has enabled a larger percentage of its citizenry to amass more wealth and possessions than any society in the history of the world. However, increased material well-being dulls moral and spiritual sensibilities.

Third, the baby-boomer generation is largely **agnostic**. America has been made to believe that truth cannot be known. Clearcut distinctions between right and wrong have been blurred. Values are now viewed as subjective and relative, rather than objective and absolute. Current culture celebrates ambiguity and uncertainty. With moral principles effectively undermined, people feel free to indulge their unfettered impulses.

Fourth, baby boomers have **an aversion to being "judgmental."** The removal of moral absolutes naturally leads to the insistence that no one take issue with anyone else's behavior. Opposition to that which is wrong is stopped dead in its tracks by a simple appeal to "you're being judgmental." Being "judgmental" (i.e., insisting that moral absolutes exist) is about the only objective wrong that exists for many Americans.

Fifth, baby boomers are **less disciplined** than the previous generation. As a result of materialism and the absence of hardship, most Americans now possess a sense of laxness and unbridled passion. Self-denial has been supplanted by self-indulgence, self-improvement, and self-esteem. Pursuit of necessities for ultimate spiritual purposes has given way to the pursuit of luxuries for physical gratification and personal fulfillment. The disciplined, self-controlled lifestyle has been replaced by the casual, unrestrained, morally bankrupt approach to life.

Sixth, baby boomers have **an insatiable craving for entertainment**. As the work ethic, so foundational to the development of American civilization, has been seriously undermined and eroded, subsequent generations have naturally occupied themselves with anything and everything that promises to relieve boredom. "Fun and games" have come to dominate the lifestyle and orientation of youth. Restlessly moving from one bauble to another, post-world war generations are engaged in a desperate attempt to find meaning and contentment through fleshly stimulation.

These and other influential social currents may be distilled into one central cultural feature that is operative in American civilization. This feature explains and accounts for everything that is happening in America that is negative, adverse, and destructive to moral and spiritual health. That one all-encompassing trait that impinges on all other factors is–**selfishness**. Let's be frank: *the baby-boomer generation, more than any previous generation, was spoiled as children*. We grew up having our every desire met. We were given an inordinate amount of trinkets and toys. Our comfort level surpassed that of the majority of the people on Earth from the beginning of human history. We cultivated our fleshly appetites by gratifying them without restraint. We want what we want. On the whole, we are a generation that is glaringly self-centered, arrogant, and selfish.

What would one logically expect to surface from this social turbulence and cultural fluctuation but much social, psychological, and moral aberration? One thing has taken place for certain: a dramatically different attitude toward sex–an attitude that has now virtually permeated American civilization. Society is literally sex-crazed–inordinately preoccupied with, and fixated on, sex. One could recount the forces that contributed to the current predicament beginning in the 1950s. In 1953, *Playboy* magazine, followed in quick succession by one pornographic magazine after another, glorified female nudity and encouraged unbridled male lust. Hollywood and the cinema industry, as well as network television, have compounded the problem by plac-

ing themselves on the cutting edge of sexual experimentation–
pushing the envelope at every opportunity, maintaining a re-
lentless assault on the standards of decency, in a mad rush to be
the first to perpetrate upon the American public loose morality
and sexual degradation. The rating system of the movie industry was formulated in the late 1960s (see "Reasons…," 2000). Yet
a movie rated "X" (now NC-17) in the Sixties is now rated "R,"
while some "R" rated movies now pass as "PG-13." In the 1950s,
a couple in their bedroom had to be in separate beds and have
one foot on the floor. Sexual behavior permitted on television
and in movies today once would have been banned and their
promoters arrested. With the advent of the Internet, pornography is even more prevalent and more easily accessible.

The sexual values of the World War II generation have been
jettisoned by baby boomers (and succeeding generations). Baby-
boomer definitions of virtue and modesty are as different from
the preceding generation as night is from day. Baby boomers
have literally overindulged themselves in the fulfillment of their
every sexual desire. The '60s motto, "If it feels good, do it," reigns
supreme.

THE CHILDREN OF THE SIXTIES
AND THE CULTURE WAR

No one can doubt that the United States of America is even
now in the throes of a full-scale culture war–a war that has been
going on for over fifty years. The war has crystallized between
two opposing forces. On the one hand, there is the "politically
correct" crowd–those who embrace pluralism, atheism, agnos-
ticism, and humanism. They generally reject the God of the Bible and the principles of morality contained therein. They define "liberty" as the right to believe in and practice whatever
they choose. "Freedom" to them means **freedom from restraint**.
They wish to be left free to indulge their fleshly appetites fully.
This indulgence has manifested itself most clearly in what was
referred to in the 1960s as the "Sexual Revolution"–the rise of

"free love," co-ed dormitories, and "shacking up," i.e., living together in a sexual relationship without being married. Many people have insisted on being unhampered in their engagement in illicit sexual activity, i.e., pre-marital, extra-marital, and homosexual sex. (The United States Supreme Court, in an unprecedented action–in direct contradiction to the stance that has completely dominated American civilization since its inception–single-handedly struck down state sodomy laws [see *Lawrence...*, 2003].) This sexual anarchy has naturally resulted in three critical cultural catastrophes–a trilogy of social terror: (1) widespread divorce and the breakdown of the home and family; (2) the legalization of abortion; and (3) the legal sanction and growing social acceptance of homosexuality as moral, normal behavior. The interpenetration of these three factors is seen in the fact that illicit sexual activity inevitably destroys marriage, and has, in turn, led to the destruction of children–either by killing them in the womb, abusing them, or neglecting to rear them properly. Most of the ills of society, and much of the present culture war, is traceable to this fundamental lack of sexual restraint.

On the other hand, there are still those in America who understand that God exists, i.e., the God of the Bible, the Creator of humanity and the Supreme Ruler of the Universe. They recognize that the Bible is His communication to humanity to instruct people how to be successful and happy in this life and how to prepare for the life to come in eternity. They recognize that American civilization must maintain its Christian foundation if it expects to survive and flourish–as it did for the 180$^+$ years preceding the current culture war.

One way to view these two opposing forces is in terms of the generational shifting that has occurred in America. The World War II generation represents the previous social atmosphere when Americans were encouraged to be "God-fearing citizens" who lived according to unchanging Christian values and the standard of the Bible. The baby-boomer generation is largely responsible for orchestrating change and igniting the culture war. The mottos of the 1960s illustrate this defiant rejection of the past:

"do your own thing," "make love, not war," "if it feels good, do it," and "the devil made me do it." Such slogans exposed the underlying intent: "I want to be left free to do **whatever I want to do**, with no restrictions and no one telling me what I can and cannot do." The present culture war is the result of the continuing attempt to be free from authority and restraint. It is the attempt to **rewrite law to make lawlessness legal!**

SEXUAL MORALITY AND THE CHRISTIAN RELIGION

Here we see what the removal of the Ten Commandments monument in Alabama in the fall of 2003 was all about. It was not about that particular monument. It was not really even about the Ten Commandments themselves. After all, the Bible teaches that God gave the Ten Commandments to Moses to govern **the Israelites** (Exodus 20:1-17). Christians have never been under the Ten Commandments *per se* (Colossians 2:14; Hebrews 9:15-17). Rather, Christians are under New Testament law brought by Christ and His apostles. Is there considerable overlap between the laws given by Moses (which included the Ten Commandments) and the laws given by Christ? Certainly. In fact, nine of the Ten Commandments (excluding the Sabbath) are repeated in one form or another in the New Testament as being a part of New Testament Christianity. The issue, then, is what constitutes the foundation of the nation. That foundation is the moral precepts latent in the Christian religion. What Alabama Supreme Court Chief Justice Roy Moore said is that the Constitution endorses the acknowledgment of the God of the Bible in public life (see "Transcript...," 2003). Note carefully what Justice Moore explained:

> Anytime you deny the acknowledgment of God you are undermining the entire basis for which our country exists. Rights come from God, not from government. If government can give you rights, government can take them away from you. If God gives you rights, no man

and no government can take them away from you. That was the premise of the organic law of this country, which is the Declaration of Independence. Because, if there is no God, then man's power is the controlling aspect, and therefore power will be centralized (as quoted in Wright, 2003).

In his monumental late-eighteenth-century work, *The History of the Decline and Fall of the Roman Empire*, Edward Gibbon offered five reasons why the Christian faith "obtained so remarkable a victory over the established religions of the earth." One of those was "the pure and austere morals of the Christians" (1776, 1.15:1). The Founding Fathers of America intended Bible morality to be the foundation of American civilization. They understood that the Republic which they founded was based upon the morality advocated in the Bible, and that the strength of the nation was dependant on adherence to that moral framework. Indeed, the "Father of our country" and first president, George Washington, articulated the point in unmistakable language in his "Farewell Address" to the nation:

> Of all the dispositions and habits which lead to political prosperity, **religion and morality** are indispensable supports. In vain would that man claim the tribute of patriotism, who should labor to subvert these great pillars of human happiness, these firmest props of the duties of men and citizens. The mere politician, equally with the pious man, ought to respect and to cherish them. A volume could not trace all their connections with private and public felicity. Let it simply be asked: Where is the security for property, for reputation, for life, if **the sense of religious obligation** desert the oaths which are the instruments of investigation in courts of justice? And let us with caution indulge the supposition that morality can be maintained **without religion**. Whatever may be conceded to the influence of refined education on minds of peculiar structure, **reason and experience both forbid us to expect that national morality can prevail in exclusion of religious principle**. It is substantially true that **virtue or morality is a necessary spring of**

popular government. The rule, indeed, extends with more or less force to every species of free government. Who that is a sincere friend to it can look with indifference upon attempts to shake the foundation of the fabric? (1796a, emp. added).

Washington was speaking of the **Christian** religion! He understood that "political prosperity" can be achieved and maintained only if the Christian religion, and the morality it enjoins, remain intact. Any other course will "shake the foundation of the fabric" of the country. Lest the reader doubt this contention, consider the following advice Washington offered in his May 12, 1779 speech to the Delaware Indian Chiefs: "You do well to wish to learn our arts and ways of life, **and above all, the religion of Jesus Christ**. These will make you a greater and happier people than you are. Congress will do everything they can to assist you in this wise intention" (1932, 15:55).

Washington was not the only Founding Father who insisted that America's survival was dependant on Christian morality. Consider the following scattered representative quotations from several of the Founders in which they declare in no uncertain terms their preference for Christianity, thereby providing evidence of their disagreement with today's alleged constitutional mandate to promote a pluralistic society in which sexual anarchy is the order of the day:

Benjamin Rush, member of the Continental Congress and signer of the *Declaration of Independence*, wrote:

> In contemplating the political institutions of the United States, I lament that we waste so much time and money in punishing crimes, and take so little pains to prevent them. We profess to be Republicans and yet we neglect the only means of establishing and perpetuating our republican forms of government; that is, **the universal education of our youth in the principles of Christianity by means of the Bible** (1798, p. 112, emp. added).

Samuel Adams, another member of the Continental Congress and signer of the *Declaration of Independence*, wrote: "Let... statesmen and patriots unite their endeavors to renovate the age by...educating their little boys and girls...[and] leading them in the study and practice of **the exalted virtues of the Christian system**" (Adams and Adams, 1802, pp. 9-10, emp. added).

Charles Carroll, yet another member of the Continental Congress, signer of the *Declaration of Independence*, and U.S. Senator, in a letter to James McHenry on November 4, 1800, wrote: "[W]ithout morals a republic cannot subsist any length of time; they therefore who are decrying **the Christian religion**, whose morality is so sublime and pure...are undermining **the solid foundation of morals**, the best security for the duration of free governments" (as quoted in Steiner, 1907, p. 475, emp. added).

Still another member of the Continental Congress and signer of the *Declaration of Independence*, William Ellery, insisted: "However gradual may be the growth of **Christian knowledge and moral reformation**, yet unless it be begun, unless the seeds are planted, there can be no tree of knowledge and, of course, no fruit. The attempt to Christianize the heathen world and to produce peace on earth and goodwill towards men is humane, Christian, and sublime" (as quoted in Sparks, 1860, 6:138-139, emp. added).

Benjamin Franklin added his agreement: "History will also afford frequent opportunities of showing the necessity of a public religion...and the excellency of **the Christian religion** above all others, ancient or modern" (1749, p. 22, emp. added).

In a letter to James Madison on October 16, 1829, Noah Webster explained: "[T]he **Christian religion**, in its purity, is the basis, or rather the source of all genuine freedom in government... and I am persuaded that no civil government of a republican form can exist and be durable in which **the principles of that religion** have not a controlling influence" (as quoted in Snyder, 1990, p. 253, emp. added).

John Witherspoon, member of the Continental Congress and signer of the *Declaration of Independence*, made the following remark in a lecture titled "On the Truth of the Christian Religion":

"[T]he **Christian religion** is superior to every other.... But there is not only an excellence in the **Christian morals**, but a manifest superiority in them to those which are derived from any other source" (1815, 8:33,38, emp. added).

John Quincy Adams, son of John Adams and sixth President of the United States, declared:

> From the day of the Declaration, the people of the North American Union and of its constituent states were associated bodies of civilized men and Christians.... They were **bound by the laws of God**, which they all, **and by the laws of the Gospel**, which they nearly all, acknowledged as **the rules of their conduct** (1821, p. 28, emp. added).

John Hancock, whose signature on the *Declaration of Independence* was the first and stands out from all others, explained:

> Sensible of the importance of **Christian piety and virtue** to the order and happiness of a state, I cannot but earnestly commend to you every measure for their support and encouragement.... Manners, by which not only the freedom **but the very existence of the republics** are greatly affected, depend much upon the public institutions of religion (as quoted in Brown, 1898, p. 269, emp. added).

In a letter to James Fishback on September 27, 1809, Thomas Jefferson affirmed:

> The practice of morality being necessary for the well-being of society, He [God–DM] has taken care to impress its precepts so indelibly on our hearts that they shall not be effaced by the subtleties of our brain. We all agree in the obligation of **the moral precepts of Jesus** and nowhere will they be found delivered in greater purity than in His discourses (1904, 12:315, emp. added).

Many additional similar declarations could be cited. Indeed, the Framers never envisioned the government being allowed to interfere with the free exercise of the Christian religion in public life (see Barton, 2000). They expected, yea, insisted that the country's longstanding religious heritage remain as the foundation of the Republic. They would surely view as **morally bankrupt and spiritually insane** the generation that would remove from one state government's premises a monument that celebrates Bible law–including sexual sanctity ("Thou shall not commit adultery")–only to install a monument on another state capitol's grounds celebrating homosexual war veterans (see Limbacher, 2003). This juxtaposition is a microcosm of the sexual anarchy that has gripped America by its moral and spiritual throat.

CHAPTER TWO

THE DEVASTATION OF DIVORCE

Since its inception, the United States of America has been a country whose Founding Fathers recognized the need for God in public life and the need for Bible principles of morality to govern and structure American society. The Founding Fathers recognized that if the country ever strayed significantly away from these foundational moral, spiritual, and ethical principles, she would be doomed as a nation. For 180$^+$ years, society recognized the importance of what some are calling the "traditional family," i.e., a husband and a wife who marry for life and rear their children together. Divorce was almost unheard of in America. When it did occur, it was regarded as deviant behavior. Family disruption in the form of separation, divorce, and out-of-wedlock birth were kept to a minimum by strong religious, social, and even legal sanctions. Immediately after World War II, most American children grew up in a family with both biological parents who were married to each other.

This state of affairs held sway up through the 1940s and 1950s. In fact, disruption of the traditional American family reached a historic low in the 1950s and early 1960s. But then something happened. Beginning in about 1965, the divorce rate suddenly skyrocketed, more than doubling over the next fifteen years. By 1974, divorce passed death as the leading cause of family breakup. By 1980, only fifty percent of children could expect to spend their entire childhood with both their parents. Now, half of all marriages end in divorce. Every year a million children are subjected to divorce or separation by their parents, and almost as many more are born out of wedlock. People who remarry after divorce are more likely to break up than couples in first marriages. The same is true for couples that just live together (see Whitehead, 1993).

Overall child well-being has declined, despite a decrease in the number of children per family, an increase in the educational level of parents, and historically high levels of public spending. Teen suicide has more than tripled. Juvenile crime has increased and become more violent. School performance has continued to decline. Some sociologists are now recognizing the incredibly harmful effect these circumstances are having on our country and the homes of America. They are beginning to realize the relationship between family structure and declining child well-being. Some are even admitting that the social arrangement that has proved most successful in ensuring the physical survival and promoting the social development of the child is the family unit of the biological mother and father.

But our society as a whole has been slow to see family disruption as a severe national problem. Why? A fundamental shift has occurred in our culture with reference to religious and moral value. Much of our society has jettisoned the Bible as the absolute standard of behavior. The Bible is no longer considered to be the authoritative regulator of daily living. Many, perhaps most, Americans no longer feel that divorce is wrong. "Irreconcilable differences" and "incompatibility" are seen as perfectly legitimate reasons for divorce—flying directly in the face of Bible teaching. Many Americans no longer feel that a couple simply living together unmarried is morally wrong. By the mid-1970s, three-fourths of Americans said that it is not morally wrong for a woman to have a child outside marriage.

The causes of this basic cultural shifting are debatable. Logically, the influence of evolution and humanism in our educational system, the impact of feminism, the increased participation of women in the work force to the neglect of their children, the widespread

THE DEVASTATION
OF DIVORCE

prosperity that we enjoy as a nation (causing us to forget God and to indulge ourselves)–these and other factors have contributed to our moral decline. Hollywood, television, and the cinema have unquestionably glamorized, defended, and promoted divorce, premarital sex, unwed motherhood, abortion, homosexuality, and the use of alcohol, obscene language, and many other immoral behaviors.

Ironically–and tragically–the media have been working overtime to discredit the married, two-parent family by playing up instances of incest, violence, and abuse. If a family has religious inclinations, its members are depicted on programs as weirdos and deviants. In fact, it is surely disgusting to the sensibilities of the morally upright that what was once mainstream and normal (i.e., the religious, church-going, two-parent family) is demonized and ridiculed, while behavior that once was considered deviant, reprehensible, and immoral is paraded before society–on TV, in the news, and in the courts–as the social norm. Anyone who lifts a finger to speak against such immorality is berated as "homophobic," "prejudiced," "judgmental," "mean-spirited," and guilty of "hate speech."

Two illustrations of the undermining of the marriage relationship as God intended are the decisions regarding homosexuality by the Episcopal Church and the United States Supreme Court. By a 62-45 vote, the Episcopal House of Bishops elected the denomination's first homosexual bishop on August 5, 2003 (see Duin, 2003). Only days earlier, the Supreme Court had ruled that sodomy laws are unconstitutional–even though sodomy was treated as a criminal offense in all of the original thirteen colonies and eventually every one of the fifty states (see Robinson, 2003; "Sodomy Laws...," 2003). The nation is now poised to accept the redefinition of marriage being advocated by the homosexual community. Sadly, a generation has arisen that simply does not share the values of its parents, grandparents, and great-grandparents. Sexual fidelity, lifelong marriage, and parenthood are simply no longer held up as worthy personal goals.

All of this self-centeredness has taken its greatest toll on the children. The erosion of basic moral values in exchange for pluralism—the growing tolerance of moral and ethical diversity, the shifting of emphasis to choice, freedom, and self-expression—have all inflicted great damage on marriage and the family, especially the children. The fuller body of empirical research now documents a number of startling conclusions:

(1) Divorce almost always brings a decline in the standard of living for the mother and children, plus a dependence on welfare; children in single-parent homes are far more likely to propagate the same behavior.

(2) Children never fully recover from divorce. Five, ten, fifteen years after a divorce, the children suffer from depression, under-achievement, and ultimately, their own troubled relationships.

(3) Young adults from disrupted families are nearly twice as likely as those from intact families to receive psychological help.

(4) Children in disrupted families are nearly twice as likely as those in intact families to drop out of high school. Those who remain in school show significant differences in educational attainment from those children who grow up in intact families.

(5) Remarriage does not reproduce nor restore the intact family structure. The latest research confirms that stepparents cannot replace the original home.

(6) For children whose parents divorced, the risk of divorce is two to three times greater than it is for children from married-parent families.

These findings—and many others—underscore the importance of both a mother and a father in fostering the emotional well-being of children (Whitehead, 1993). But even more far-reaching effects have been documented—effects that impact society at large beyond the confines of the family. Authorities now are beginning to admit that a central cause of our most pressing social problems (i.e., poverty, crime, and school performance) is the breakup of the traditional American family.

THE DEVASTATION
OF DIVORCE

What is even more startling is the fact that as an institution, marriage has lost much of its legal, religious, and social meaning and authority. For most of American history, marriage was one of the most important rites of passage in life. But now, marriage has lost much of its role and significance as a rite of passage. Sex is increasingly detached from the promise or expectation of marriage. Cohabitation has emerged as a prominent experience for young adults–replacing marriage as the first living-together union. It is estimated that a quarter of unmarried women between the ages of 25 and 39 are currently living with a partner, and about half have lived at some time with an unmarried partner. Referring to this state of affairs as "the deinstitutionalization of marriage," researchers at the National Marriage Project at Rutgers University concluded: "Taken together, the marriage indicators do not argue for optimism about a quick or widespread come-back of marriage. Persistent long-term trends suggest a steady weakening of marriage as a lasting union, a major stage in the adult life course, and as the primary institution governing child-bearing and parenthood" (Popenoe and Whitehead, 1999).

Make no mistake: the social science evidence clearly documents the fact that the breakdown of the traditional two-parent, biological husband-wife family is a major factor contributing to the overall moral, religious, and ethical decline of our country. The social fabric of American civilization is literally tearing apart. The social arrangement that has proved most successful in ensuring the physical survival, and promoting the social development, of the child is the family unit of the biological mother and father. America is in deep trouble.

Society is not likely to solve these massive problems. The liberal elite has been operating with great vigor for over forty years to push our country into "value neutrality" and "political correctness." The clear-cut restraints and distinctions between right and wrong so typical of American culture in the past have been systematically dismantled. Relativism has taken the place of objective, absolute truth. The glorification of the individual has encouraged people to determine for themselves right and wrong–

rather than looking outside themselves to the Transcendent Creator of the Universe. Consequently, whatever the individual feels is right is sanctioned as right—at least for that individual. Even otherwise religious persons now try to justify their marital and sexual decisions on the basis of "God wants me to be happy and divorcing my mate and marrying another will make me happy." The absolute standard of moral value and human behavior—which previously governed the nation—has been successfully supplanted. Subjectivity reigns supreme, and God has been effectively severed from human culture. "Everyone did what was right in his own eyes" (Judges 21:12).

DIVORCE AND THE WILL OF GOD

The solution to rampant divorce is to be found in only one place, and no other. Only the Creator of human beings and the Author of the marriage relationship is in the position to provide ultimate counsel. What is the Creator's view of marriage and divorce? A very simple and succinct statement from God Himself, given at the very beginning of the human race, sets the tone and tenor for all of humanity for all time. After creating the first male of the species, and noting that it was not good that the man should be alone (Genesis 2:18), He created for Adam a helper that was suitable for him—fashioned from his own body. When she was brought to the man, he commented: "This is now bone of my bones, and flesh of my flesh; she shall be called Woman, because she was taken out of Man" (Genesis 2:23). God, then articulated the foundational building block for human civilization: "Therefore a man shall leave his father and mother and be joined to his wife, and they shall become one flesh" (Genesis 2:24).

In that one sweeping declaration, God's will concerning marriage for all human beings on the face of the Earth was set forth. The Divine desire is that there be **one man** who marries **one woman for life**. That is God's general marriage law. It has existed since the very beginning of Creation, when He placed the first human beings on the Earth in the Garden of Eden.

THE DEVASTATION
OF DIVORCE

If sexual anarchy is to be arrested, a return to the high standards given by God must be achieved. Citizens across the country must come to understand and embrace the fact that God's will regarding sex and marriage is that a man marry a woman, and the two remain married all the days of their life. This foundational plank of God's will for humanity is, in fact, the one and only way to achieve marital happiness and sexual satisfaction. To be genuinely happy, to avoid the grief, despair, heartache, and unhappiness brought about by illicit sexual activity, one must listen closely to what God says on the matter. His ideal will is that an unmarried male marry an unmarried female (neither having been previously married), and that the two of them, man and woman, remain married for the rest of their lives: one man, for one woman, for life. God's will for human beings is actually simple. Those who wish to be happy must respect that simple but profound law of marriage given by the Creator of human sexuality.

When humans circumvent the Divine will and entangle themselves in illicit sexual relationships, the only solution is to extricate themselves from those relationships (see Ezra 9-10). A marital relationship that is formed in conflict with God's will must be dissolved (Ezra 10:3,11). Applying divine sexual principles to one's life may well be emotionally painful and physically trying. Nevertheless, God knows best. Being the Creator Who made us, He knows what will bring ultimate and final fulfillment, happiness, and contentment. But one must muster enough devotion to God, enough confidence in God, and enough faith in the Word of God to comply, by sacrificing one's immediate sexual and emotional preferences, thereby achieving favor with God.

Notice carefully that God linked sex with marriage. In order to enjoy sexual relations, and to achieve true sexual satisfaction, one must marry permanently (i.e., "till death parts us"), and marry correctly (i.e., in harmony with God's directives). Sexual relationships within such a marriage would be truly satisfying. If a marriage is contracted out of harmony with the will of God, God requires that marriage relationship to end.

On the other hand, when a marriage has been contracted that is in harmony with God's will, that marriage must **not** be dissolved (with one exception noted below). The ancient Hebrew prophet Malachi described how the men of his day divorced their wives for no acceptable reason, and were marrying younger women. He charged them with an offense against God, and even stated forthrightly that "the Lord God of Israel says that He hates divorce" (Malachi 2:16). That pronouncement is very clear–though it stands in stark contrast to the rampant divorce that exists in American society. Nevertheless, God does not want people to divorce. He does not want them to dissolve a scriptural marriage. Should they do so, He does not permit them to marry other spouses. It is God's will that marriage be **permanent**. Literally millions of men, women, and children could have been spared great heartache and grief if the adults would recognize and honor this fundamental principle of human existence, given by God Himself. The rampant divorce in society has inflicted great emotional suffering and psychological scars on millions of children–permanent damage created by essentially thoughtless, self-centered mothers and fathers who chose to terminate their marriages, though those marriages were approved by God.

JESUS' VIEW

Jesus Christ Himself addressed this significant matter. Certain Jewish leaders approached Him and posed a question: "Is it lawful for a man to divorce his wife for just any reason?" (Matthew 19:3). The answer to that question from the viewpoint and practice of American civilization since 1965 would have to be a resounding "yes!" But is God pleased with that answer? Is it scripturally acceptable to God for a person to divorce his or her scriptural mate for whatever reason they choose? Jesus' answer to the question was simple, direct, and unflinching. He reached back to the very passage noted above–God's directive at the very beginning of time found in Genesis 2:24. Jesus quoted the statement, leaving the impression that the answer to their question was, "no." It is **not** legal, lawful, or acceptable to God to divorce one's mate for any and every reason. He then applied that original divine principle to the specific question of divorce: "I say to you, whoever divorces his wife, except for sexual immorality, and marries another, commits adultery." Keep in mind that Jesus Christ was declaring His own Word on the matter.

It is clear from the context that Jesus was simply reiterating what had **always** been God's will on the matter of divorce. God has always wanted the man to stay married to his first wife for life. The only exception, the only allowance made by God, in which a man may put away that first wife and form a second marriage (while his first wife is still living), is if, and only if, that man's first wife commits **fornication**. On that ground, and that ground alone, God and Jesus permit a second marriage for the innocent spouse.

This legislation makes clear that the person who divorces the initial scriptural mate, for some reason other than that mate's fornication, and marries again, is guilty of committing adultery. And the Bible is very clear about God's view concerning those who commit adultery and who remain in an adulterous relationship till death without repenting (see Hebrews 13:4; Revelation 21:8).

But what is "fornication"? This seemingly complicated word is quite easily defined according to the Bible. The term fornication in the original Greek (i.e., *porneia*) refers to "every kind of unlawful sexual intercourse" (Arndt and Gingrich, 1957, p. 699) or "illicit sexual intercourse in general" (Thayer, 1901, p. 532). If a person's mate is sexually unfaithful to the marriage relationship by engaging in sexual intercourse with another partner, be it male or female, that person is guilty of fornication. The innocent party has the scriptural right, if he or she chooses to exercise that right, to divorce the unfaithful mate **on the sole grounds of that sexual infidelity**, and then to contract a second legitimate, scriptural marriage. Of course, an individual would not have to exercise that scriptural right. He or she could choose to exercise the equally scriptural principle of forgiveness, long-suffering, patience, and endurance, and keep the marriage intact. Nevertheless, Jesus Christ grants the opportunity of a second marriage to the **innocent** partner, but only upon the ground of fornication (sexual unfaithfulness on the part of the guilty partner).

PAUL'S VIEW

In a discussion of the Christian's relationship to the obsolete, expired Law of Moses, Paul made an analogy using the marriage relationship.

> Or do you not know, brethren (for I speak to those who know the law), that the law has dominion over a man as long as he lives? For the woman who has a husband is bound by the law to her husband as long as he lives. But if the husband dies, she is released from the law of her husband. So then if, while her husband lives, she marries another man, she will be called an adulteress; but if her husband dies, she is free from that law, so that she is no adulteress, though she has married another man (Romans 7:1-3).

The apostle made it clear that a woman is free from the marriage relationship with her husband, and consequently free to form another marriage relationship, if her first husband is dead. The death of her first husband frees her from that marriage relationship, releasing her to form a second sexual union without being guilty of committing adultery.

In another context, Paul reiterated the very thing that Jesus taught in Matthew 19: "Now to the married I command, yet not I but the Lord: A wife is not to depart from her husband. But even if she does depart, let her remain unmarried or be reconciled to her husband. And a husband is not to divorce his wife" (1 Corinthians 7:10-12). Husbands and wives are not to divorce each other without the one scriptural ground of fornication. If they do break up their marriage for some unscriptural reason, they must refrain from compounding their sin of divorce by forming another marriage. Rather, they are to remain unmarried or be reconciled to the original marriage partner.

The writer of Hebrews was equally adamant in his insistence that sexual sin will cause many people to be lost at the Judgment when he declared: "Marriage is honorable among all, and the bed undefiled; but fornicators and adulterers God will judge" (Hebrews 13:4). His words constitute an admonition and exhortation, indeed, a command that God's will concerning sex be observed. Two people who initially marry scripturally must sustain that marriage relationship for the rest of their lives. The only way that their marriage relationship can end, as far as God is concerned, is if one spouse dies, or if one spouse is unfaithful sexually. Where fornication is the cause, the innocent mate (not the guilty mate) has the right to dissolve that marriage and form a second marriage. Those who fail to observe what God says on this matter–thereby engaging in fornication and adultery–"God will judge."

To summarize, the Bible teaches very clearly that it is God's will for every human being on the face of the Earth who chooses to marry, to marry an eligible person, and the two must remain married until death ends the relationship. The only way God will allow either of the two persons to end their marriage prior to the death of either one, and to form a second marriage relationship, is if the innocent mate divorces the sexually unfaithful mate on the sole ground of sexual infidelity. God permits the innocent spouse the right of remarriage. This is God's will for every human being. Those who divorce and remarry in violation of divine precepts must extricate themselves from their illicit sexual entanglements, bringing their lives into harmony with God's directives. John issued a most sober warning: "[T]he sexually immoral...shall have their part in the lake which burns with fire and brimstone" (Revelation 21:8). Marriage, divorce, and sexual relations are extremely serious matters. In fact, this issue is of such paramount importance to God that when John the Baptizer "stuck to his guns" by insisting that King Herod was living in violation of God's marriage directives, he paid for it with his head (Mark 6:14-29).

NATIONAL NEGLECT

Americans now virtually **ignore** God's will on these matters. **In less than thirty years, divorce has gone from being rare to routine**. Not only is the baby-boomer generation virtually certain to become the first generation for which a majority experienced a divorce, with successive generations following close behind, popular pollster, George Barna, has two startling statistics to stomach: those in America who claim to be Christians have the same likelihood of divorce as do non-Christians, and a majority of Christians disagree that divorce without adultery is sin ("Born Again...," 2004).

Indeed, Americans now feel free to marry, divorce, remarry, divorce again, remarry again—all for reasons that the law of the land allows, but which God Himself does not allow. Large numbers of Americans engage in sexual relations without even being married—let alone being married scripturally. Incredibly, in one of America's premiere public school textbooks in 1857, the following observation appeared: "It was once a practice in France to divorce husband and wife **for incompatibility** of tempers; a practice soon found to be **incompatible with social order**" (Webster, 1857, p. 113, emp. added)

One must ask oneself: "Do I want to go to heaven? Do I want to go to heaven more than anything in this life? Do I want to go to heaven to the point that I will deny myself and deprive myself of momentary sexual pleasure in this life?" God so requires. He holds every human being on the face of the Earth to the same standard. We simply must not allow our marital choices and our desire for sexual relationships to interfere with our relationship with God, thereby preventing us from entering into heaven.

People are permitted to participate in marriage only insofar as God says they are eligible to do so. After all, God is the Author of marriage, and He is the One who actually joins people together in marriage. The Hebrews writer insisted that marriage (and the sexual relationship that accompanies marriage) is to be undertaken **honorably**—i.e., in accordance with God's regulations. To engage in marriage (and the sexual relations that accompany marriage) out of harmony with God's regulations is to be guilty of fornication and adultery (Hebrews 13:4). A person does not **have** to be married in order to please God and go to heaven. All a person **has** to be is a Christian. A person does not have to be a preacher. He or she does not have to be a parent. These are relationships and roles that God designed to be helpful to the human condition. However, not everyone qualifies to fill these roles, and people can go to heaven without ever occupying these roles. So it is with marriage. All people must meet God's designated prerequisites before marriage may be had **in honor**. God nowhere promises anyone unlimited access to a sexual relationship.

Many people feel that such strict limitations are out of harmony with the grace, love, and forgiveness of God. They believe that such high standards make divorce the "unpardonable sin." But this conclusion does not follow. People can be forgiven of mistakes they make in the realm of divorce and remarriage. Forgiveness is not the issue. **The issue is: can they remain in whatever marriage relationship they choose?** And can they so sin that they forfeit their right to participate in a future marriage relationship? Jesus made the answers to these questions clear in His discussion in Matthew 19:1-12. All people who divorce their scriptural mates for any reason except fornication continue to commit adultery when they remarry.

Does the Bible teach that people can so sin that they **forfeit** their privilege to participate in a state, condition, or relationship that they previously enjoyed–even though they may be forgiven? As a matter of fact, the Bible is replete with such instances. Adam and Eve violated God's Word and were responsible for introducing sin into the Universe. One consequence of their sin was that they were expelled from Eden. Could they be forgiven? Yes! Could they ever return to the garden? **No!** Their expulsion was **permanent**. They had so sinned that they forfeited the privilege of enjoying that previous status.

Esau was guilty of profanity when he sold his birthright (Genesis 25:33). Could he be forgiven for this mistake? Yes! Could he regain his birthright and the blessing? **No**—"though he sought it diligently with tears" (Hebrews 12:17; Genesis 27:34,38). Virtually the entire adult population of the nation of Israel sinned when they refused to obey God by proceeding with a military assault against the land of Canaan (Numbers 14:11-12). Could they be forgiven? Yes, and they were (Numbers 14:19-20). Were they then permitted to enter into the Promised Land? Absolutely **not**! They were doomed to wander in the desert for forty years and die there (Numbers 14:33-34).

Moses allowed himself to be goaded into disobedience on one occasion by the incessant complaining of the nation committed to his keeping (Numbers 20:7-12). Could Moses be forgiven? Yes! In heaven, the song of Moses and the Lamb will be sung (Revelation 15:3). But was Moses permitted to enter into the Promised Land? No. He was permanently banned from that privilege due to his own sinful choice (Deuteronomy 32:51-52).

Eli failed to manage his family properly, and so brought down upon himself lasting tragedies (1 Samuel 3:11-14). Though Saul acknowledged his own sin, his disobedience evoked God's permanent rejection of him as king (1 Samuel 15:11,23,26,28). Samuel never visited Saul again. David's sin, though forgiven, brought several negative consequences that could not be altered (2 Samuel 12:11-14). Solomon's sin resulted in personal calamity and the division of the nation (1 Kings 11-12).

These biblical examples demonstrate that sin produces **lasting** consequences, despite the availability of God's grace and forgiveness. If biblical history teaches anything, it teaches that people cannot sin and then expect to have things the way they were before. More often than not, much suffering comes upon those who violate God's will, making it **impossible** for them to enjoy past privileges—though they can be forgiven and have the hope of heaven.

THE DEVASTATION
OF DIVORCE

Many people feel that God would be unkind, unfair, or overly harsh if He did not permit divorced and remarried couples to stay together, regardless of their previous marital choices. Undoubtedly, these same people would feel that God was unfair to Adam and Eve for ejecting them from Eden, making it impossible for them to enjoy any further the blissful habitat of the garden. That would mean that God was unfair and harsh toward the Israelites as well as Moses. Such thinking betrays an inaccurate and unscriptural grasp of **the nature and person of God**. It also reflects a failure to possess a healthy fear of God and respect for His Word (Exodus 20:5; Ecclesiastes 12:13-14; Luke 12:5; 2 Thessalonians 1:8-9; Hebrews 10:31; 12:29; Revelation 6:16-17).

Many apparently feel that they have a right to be married regardless of their previous conduct. They feel that God's high standards ought to be adjusted in order for them to exercise their "right." Yet, the Bible teaches that the institution of marriage was founded by God to provide cohesion and orientation in life. Unlike one's spiritual marriage (i.e., to Christ), which will proceed right on into eternity, human marriage is for this life alone (Matthew 22:30). Therefore, **marriage is not a right; it is a privilege**. People must conform to God's marriage rules in order for marriage to serve its earthly purpose. Failure to comply neutralizes the ability of the marriage institution to do what it was divinely designed to do. Failure to comply with God's "directions for use" disqualifies the user, and causes the individuals involved to forfeit their opportunity to participate in the institution. We must remember: Father knows best.

CONCLUSION

The Bible is too clear on this matter. Due to prior marital decisions and sexual behavior, those who have lived their lives out of harmony with Bible teaching may well have to forfeit the right to any future participation in marriage and sex. This circumstance may result in what is deemed to be unbearable agony, sorrow, grief, loneliness, and deprivation. But it can be done. God's will can be obeyed. It has always been the case for human beings throughout time, that in order to obey God and be pleasing to Him, many times deeply painful sacrifices must be made.

For example, Moses chose "rather **to suffer affliction** with the people of God than to enjoy the passing pleasures of sin" (Hebrews 11:25, emp. added). A person may very well have to live a lonely, celibate lifestyle, being deprived of the marriage relationship, in order to be right with God and live eternally with Him.

The church in Corinth had members who had been fornicators—including adulterers and homosexuals. During their pre-Christian lives, they had involved themselves in sexual relationships that were unlawful in God's sight—relationships that they had no right to contract or persist in. But they could still receive the approval of God. When Paul said, "such **were** some of you" (1 Corinthians 6:11), it is evident that they had ended those unlawful relationships. They had put an end to those illicit sexual relationships and brought their sexual behavior into line with God's will.

While American civilization has moved so very far away from the standard of marital and sexual behavior dictated by God, the social environment can be reversed—if each individual decides to do so. It is imperative that a person love God enough to obey His will. It is not always easy to obey God. Jesus Himself said that it may mean turning one's back on parents, children, husbands, or wives (Matthew 10:35-37). But is it too much to ask to live with God forever? Is it too much to ask in light of the great sacrifice that He made for us?

CHAPTER
THREE

THE ABOMINATION
OF ABORTION

As traditional values (i.e., **biblical** values) continue to be systematically extracted from American culture, moral and spiritual confusion have been the inevitable result. This disorientation is particularly evident in the passionately held, conflicting viewpoints of the abortion controversy. On Monday, January 22, 1973, the United States Supreme Court ruled, in a 7-to-2 vote, that abortion would be legalized and made available on demand throughout America. Such abortions, stated the Court's edict, could be performed up to and including the ninth month, with the doctor's permission, if the physical or mental health of the prospective mother was deemed "at risk." Consider the following excerpts from the court's majority opinion: "All this...persuades us that **the word 'person,'** as used in the Fourteenth Amendment, **does not include the unborn**.... There has always been strong support for the view that **life does not begin until live birth**.... In short, **the unborn have never been recognized in the law as persons** in the whole sense" (see *Roe v. Wade*, emp. added). Yet, all relevant scientific information points to one conclusion: a pre-born infant is a human being–a person (see Thompson, 2004, pp. 166-168).

Since that fateful and infamous judicial decision, more than **45 million babies have been slaughtered** in America (see "Abortion in the...," 2005). That number is 10 million more than the population of the entire state of California–the most populous state! It is approximately 16 percent (or one-sixth) of the current U.S. population! Imagine exterminating the entire resident populations of the following states: Alaska, Arkansas, Connecticut, Delaware, Hawaii, Idaho, Iowa, Kansas, Maine, Mississippi, Montana, Nebraska, Nevada, New Hampshire, New Mexico, North Dakota, Oklahoma, Oregon, South Carolina, South Dakota, Utah, Vermont, West Virginia, and Wyoming–24 states (see "Resident Population...," 2000)! Every year in America, abortion doctors butcher more than one million children. Every year, an estimated 46 million abortions occur worldwide (Alan Guttmacher Institute, 2002). In three decades, an entire generation of children has been forever eliminated. In fact, more than 20% of all babies conceived in this country are killed before they ever see the light of day (Finer and Henshaw, 2003, p. 6), and the horrendous slaughter continues.

Some encouraging signs have surfaced in recent years. Though President Bill Clinton twice vetoed the measure during his administration, in March 2003, the United States Senate, by a 64-33 vote, approved a ban on the particularly barbaric abortion procedure known as "partial-birth" abortion (Kiely, 2003). In June, the House passed a similar bill. By October, amid liberals' fears of a possible overturning of *Roe v. Wade*, both sides were predicting the finalization of the law (Fagan, 2003). Though on November 5, 2003, President Bush signed the Partial Birth Abortion Act into law, by June 1, 2004, U.S. District Court Judge Phyllis Hamilton ruled the act an unconstitutional infringement on a woman's right to choose (see "Judge Blocks...," 2004). Another encouraging sign was seen, when, in their efforts to sort out the moral and ethical issues involved in human cloning, members of the President's Council on Bioethics concluded, among other things, that "the case for treating the early-stage embryo as simply the moral equivalent of all other human cells...is simply mistaken" (Kass, 2002, p. liv). But, sadly, the laudable attempts to turn back the tide of moral degradation that has swept over the nation appear to be too little, too late.

Unfortunately, a majority of Americans consider abortion to be a morally acceptable option (see "Abortion," 2004). What would one expect? They've been browbeaten with the "politically correct" propaganda agenda of social liberals for decades. The highest court in the land has weighed in on the matter, making abortion legitimate by means of the power of "the law." The medical profession has followed suit, lending its prestige and sanction to the practice of abortion—in direct violation of the Hippocratic Oath. The original version of the oath read: "I will give no deadly medicine to any one if asked, nor suggest any such counsel; and in like manner **I will not give a woman a pessary to produce abortion**" (see "The Hippocratic Oath," emp. added). [NOTE: Medical schools in America are not required to administer oaths to their graduates. Hence, what oaths are administered, if any, vary from school to school (Gersten, n.d.).]

American civilization has undergone a sweeping cultural revolution during the last forty years. The American moral framework is being restructured, and this country's religious roots and spiritual perspective are being altered. Most of the Founding Fathers, and the American population of the first 180^+ years of our national existence, would not have tolerated many of the beliefs and practices that have become commonplace in society. In fact, during those years the courts consistently ruled in favor of Christian morals and values (e.g., *Updegraph v. The Commonwealth* [1824]; *The Commonwealth v. Sharpless* [1815]; *Davis v. Beason* [1889]). This list of practices would include gambling (i.e., lottery, horse racing, casinos, etc.), divorce, drunkenness, homosexuality, unwed pregnancy, and pornography in movies and magazines. These behaviors simply would not have been tolerated by the bulk of American society from the beginning up to World War II. But the moral and religious foundations of our nation are experiencing catastrophic erosion. The widespread practice of abortion is simply one sign among many of this cultural shift in our country. Another is the estimated two to five thousand children who die annually in America as a result of abuse and neglect ("Child Fatalities...," 2003).

But there is still a God in heaven–the omnipotent, omniscient Creator of the Universe. He has stated in His Word that He one day will call to account all human beings who have ever lived, and He will judge them on the basis of their behavior on Earth. Therefore, every single person is responsible for carefully studying God's Word, determining how He wants humans to behave, and complying with those directions. It is that simple, and it is that certain. Have the majority of Americans heard the **biblical** viewpoint? Do they even care how **God** feels about abortion? Are they interested in investigating **His** view of the matter? After all, the Bible does, in fact, speak decisively about abortion.

ABORTION AND THE WILL OF GOD

While the Bible does not speak **directly** to the practice of abortion, it does provide enough relevant material to enable us to know God's will on the matter. In Zechariah 12:1, God is said to be not only the Creator of the heavens and the Earth, but also the One Who "forms the spirit of man within him." So God is the giver of life. That fact alone makes human life sacred. God is responsible for implanting the human spirit within the body. Humans have no right to end human life–unless God authorizes them to do so. Taking a human life, biblically, must be based on that human's **behavior**. Taking the life of an unborn infant certainly is not based upon the moral conduct of that infant. So if God places the human spirit in a human being while that person is in the mother's womb, to end that life constitutes a deliberate interference with God's previous action of having formed the spirit of man within, and amounts to murder.

But **when** does the human spirit enter the human body and thereby bring into existence a human being? When does God implant the soul into the body–at birth or prior to birth? The Bible provides abundant evidence to answer that question. For example, Solomon stated: "As you do not know how the spirit comes to the bones **in the womb** of a woman with child, so you do not know the work of God who makes everything" (Ecclesiastes 11: 5, RSV, emp. added). In this passage, the Bible equates fetal development and infusion of the spirit with the activity of God. Job described the same process in Job 10:11-12. There he attributed his own pre-birth growth to God. David was even more specific.

> For You have formed my inward parts; You have covered me **in my mother's womb**. I will praise You, for I am fearfully and wonderfully made; marvelous are Your works, and that my soul knows very well. My frame was not hidden from You, when I was made in secret, and skillfully wrought in the lowest parts of the earth. Your eyes saw my substance, being yet unformed. And in Your book they all were written, the days fashioned for me, when as yet there were none of them (Psalm 139:13-16, emp. added).

David insisted that his development as a human being—his personhood—was achieved **by God, prior** to his birth, while he was yet in his mother's womb. Some have suggested that Ecclesiastes, Job, and Psalms are all books of poetry and, therefore, not to be taken literally. However, **poetic language has meaning**. Solomon, Job, and David clearly attributed their **pre-birth personhood** to the creative activity of God.

Jeremiah declared: "Then the word of the Lord came unto me, saying: 'Before I formed you in the womb I knew you; **before you were born** I sanctified you; and I ordained you a prophet to the nations' " (Jeremiah 1:4-5, emp. added). Compare this statement with Paul's equivalent claim, in which he said that God set him apart to do his apostolic ministry even while he was in his mother's womb (Galatians 1:15). Isaiah made the same declaration: "Listen, O coastlands, to me, and take heed, you peoples from afar! The Lord has called me from the womb; from the matrix of my mother He has made mention of my name" (Isaiah 49:1).

These passages do not teach the Calvinistic doctrine of pre-destination. Jeremiah and Paul could have exercised their free will and rejected God's will for their lives—in which case God would have found someone else to do the job. But these passages do teach that God treats people as human beings even **before** they are born, and that He has a plan for every individual—should they choose to live it. These passages show that a pre-born infant is a **person**—a human being. There is no significant difference between a human one minute **before** birth, and that same human one minute **after** birth. That status as a human being applies to a person throughout his or her prenatal development from the moment of conception. Indeed, since a baby's body is alive in the womb (a fact admitted by the medical community), and since a body is not alive without its spirit (James 2:26), it follows that the baby's spirit is present during the nine months that precede birth (McCord, n.d., 2:368).

Consider further the recorded visit that Mary, the mother of Jesus, made to Elizabeth, the mother of John the Baptizer. Both women were pregnant at the time.

> Now Mary arose in those days and went into the hill country with haste, to a city of Judah, and entered the house of Zacharias and greeted Elizabeth. And it happened, when Elizabeth heard the greeting of Mary, that **the babe leaped in her womb**; and Elizabeth was filled with the Holy Spirit. Then she spoke out with a loud voice and said, "Blessed are you among women, and blessed is the fruit of your womb! But why is this granted to me, that the mother of my Lord should come to me? For indeed, as soon as the voice of your greeting sounded in my ears, **the babe leaped in my womb** for joy" (Luke 1:39-44, emp. added).

Notice that Elizabeth's pre-born infant is being represented as a living human being. In fact, the term "babe" (*brephos*) used in verses 41 and 44 to refer to the pre-born John is the exact same term that is used in the next chapter to refer to Jesus **after** His birth as He lay in the manger (Luke 2:12,16). So in **God's** sight, whether a person is in his or her **pre**-birth developmental state, or in a **post**-birth developmental state, that person is still a baby! In Luke 1:36, John the Baptizer is referred to as "a son" from the very moment of **conception through six months of pre-birth growth**. All three phases of human life are listed in reverse order in Hosea 9:11–birth, pregnancy, and conception.

If abortion is not wrong, Mary would have been within her moral and spiritual rights to abort the baby Jesus–the divine Son of God! God would not have made abortion wrong for Mary and right for everyone else. Someone may say, "But that's different, since God had a special plan for that child." But the Bible teaches that God has special plans for **every** human being. Every single human life is precious to God–so much so that a single soul is more significant than everything else that is physical in the world (Matthew 16:26). God sacrificed His own Son for every single human being on an **individual** basis. Each human life is equally valuable to God. The unrealized and incomprehensible potential of millions of human beings has been forever expunged by abortion. The remarkably resourceful potential of even one of those tiny human minds–now extinguished–may well have included a cure for cancer, or some other horrible, debilitating, and deadly disease.

Another insightful passage from the Old Testament is Exodus 21:22-25, which describes what action is to be taken in a case of **accidental**, or at least coincidental, injury to a pregnant woman:

> If men fight, and hurt a woman with child, so that she gives birth prematurely, yet no lasting harm follows, he shall surely be punished accordingly as the woman's husband imposes on him; and he shall pay as the judges determine. But if any lasting harm follows, then you shall give life for life, eye for eye, tooth for tooth, hand for hand, foot for foot, burn for burn, wound for wound, stripe for stripe (NKJV).

Several features of this passage require clarification. First, the NKJV and NIV rendering of the underlying Hebrew as "she gives birth prematurely," and the KJV and ASV rendering "so that her fruit depart (from her)" are accurate reflections of the original. "Fruit" in the KJV is the noun form of a verb that means "to bring forth (children)" (Schreiner, 1990, 6:76; Harris, et al., 1980, 1: 378-379). Thus the noun form (*yeled*), used 89 times in the Old Testament, refers to that which is brought forth, i.e., children, and is generally so translated (Gesenius, 1847, p. 349; Wigram, 1890, 530-531; cf. VanGemeren, 1997, 2:457). For example, it is used to refer to Ishmael (Genesis 21:8), Moses (Exodus 2:3), Obed, the child of Boaz and Ruth (Ruth 4:16), and even to the Christ child (Isaiah 9:6). It is used in the same context earlier in the chapter to refer to the children born to a Hebrew servant whose wife was provided by his master (Exodus 21:4). There is nothing in the word itself that indicates the physical condition of the child/children, whether dead or alive (cf. 2 Samuel 12:14-23).

Second, the term translated "prematurely" or "depart" (*yatsa*) is a Hebrew verb that has the broad meaning of "to go out, to go forth" (Gesenius, p. 359). It is used in the Old Testament to refer to everything from soldiers going forth to war (1 Samuel 8:20) or the Sun going forth in its rising (Genesis 19:23), to a flower blossoming (Job 14:2) or the birth of a child (Job 1:21). The Hebrew is as generic as the English words "to go out or forth." As with *yeled*, there is nothing in the word itself that would imply the physical status of the child–whether unharmed, injured, or dead (cf. Numbers 12:12; Deuteronomy 28:57). For example, referring to the births of Esau and Jacob, the text reads: "And the first **came out** red...Afterward his brother **came out**" (Genesis 25:25-26, emp. added). Only by contextual details may one determine the condition of the child.

Consequently, in Exodus 21:22, those translations that render the Hebrew as "miscarriage" (e.g., NASB, RSV, NEB) have taken a linguistically unwarranted and indefensible liberty with the text. Hebrew lexicographers Brown, Driver, and Briggs were accurate in their handling of the underlying Hebrew when they listed Exodus 21:22 as an instance of "untimely birth" (1906, p. 423).

In contrast, the Hebrew had other words more suited to pinpointing a miscarriage or stillbirth. For example, suffering Job moaned: "Or why was I not hidden like **a stillborn child**, like infants who never saw light?" (Job 3:16, emp. added). The psalmist pronounces imprecation against unrighteous judges: "Let them be like a snail which melts away as it goes, like **a stillborn child** of a woman, that they may not see the sun" (Psalm 58:8, emp. added). The word used in these verses (*nephel*), occurring only three times in the Old Testament (cf. Ecclesiastes 6:3-5), is defined by Gesenius as "a premature birth, which falls from the womb, an abortion" (p. 558; cf. Brown, et al., p. 658). In all three contexts, a miscarriage or stillbirth is clearly under consideration.

Still another Hebrew term would have been more suitable to identify deceased offspring. When Jacob protested his father-in-law's unkindness, he exclaimed, "These twenty years I have been with you; your ewes and your female goats have not **miscarried their young**" (Genesis 31:38, emp. added; cf. Job 21:10). Hosea called upon God to punish the nation: "Give them a **miscarrying womb** and dry breasts!" (Hosea 9:14, emp. added). In fact, just two chapters after the text in question, God announced to the Israelites details regarding the conquest of Canaan and the blessings that they would enjoy: "No one shall suffer **miscarriage** or be barren in your land; I will fulfill the number of your days" (Exodus 23:26, emp. added). The underlying Hebrew verb in these verses (*shachol*) means "to cause abortion (in women, flocks, etc.)" or "to make abortion, i.e., to suffer it" (Gesenius, p. 822; cf. Brown, et al. p. 1013). Despite these more precise terms to pinpoint miscarriage or stillbirth, Moses did not use them in Exodus 21:22.

Third, consider the next phrase in the verse: "yet no lasting harm follows" (NKJV), "but there is no serious injury" (NIV), "and yet no harm follow" (ASV). These English renderings capture the Hebrew accurately. Absolutely no grammatical indication exists in the text by which one could assume the recipient of the injury to be either the mother or the child to the exclusion of the other. As Fishbane observed: "It is syntactically and grammatically unclear whether the object of the 'calamity' is the foetus or the pregnant mother" (1985, p. 93). In order to allow Scripture to stand on its own and speak for itself, one must conclude that to understand "injury" to refer exclusively to the mother is to narrow the meaning without textual justification.

Hence, one is forced to conclude that the absence of specificity was deliberate on the part of the inspired writer, and that he intended for the reader to conclude that the prescription applied to **both** mother and child. The wording, therefore, is the most appropriate and economical if the writer intended to convey all possible scenarios without having to go into tedious elaboration—which would have included at least the following eight combinations: (1) non-lethal injury to the child but no injury to the mother; (2) non-lethal injury to the mother but no injury to the child; (3) non-lethal injury to both; (4) death to the child but no injury to the mother; (5) death to the child with non-lethal injury to the mother; (6) death to the mother with no injury to the child; (7) death to the mother with non-lethal injury to the child; and (8) death to both mother and child.

Old Testament scholar Gleason Archer Jr. summarized the point of the passage:

> What is required is that if there should be an injury either to the mother **or to her children**, the injury shall be avenged by a like injury to the assailant. If it involves the life (*ne-peš*) of **the premature baby**, then the assailant shall pay for it with his life. There is no second-class status attached to the fetus under this rule (1982, p. 248, emp. added).

Numerous scholars agree with this assessment of the text. Responding to the poor translation of the Hebrew by the Septuagint, and the corresponding misconception of the Alexandrian Jew, Philo, Keil and Delitzsch correctly countered: "But the arbitrary character of this explanation is apparent at once; for *yeled* only denotes a child, as a fully developed human being, and not the fruit of the womb before it has assumed a human form" (1976, pp. 134-135). They also insist that the structure of the Hebrew phraseology "apparently renders it impracticable to refer the words to injury done to the woman alone" (p. 135). Walter Kaiser noted: "For the accidental assault, the offender must still pay some compensation, even though both mother **and child** survived.... Should the pregnant woman **or her child** die, the principle of *talio* is invoked, demanding 'life for life'" (1990, 2:434, emp. added). In view of this understanding of the text, under Mosaic Law "the unborn child would be considered viable *in utero* and entitled to legal protection and benefits" (Fishbane, p. 93).

In his *Treatise on the Soul* (ch. 37), Tertullian (who died c. A.D. 220) alluded to this passage in Exodus 21:

> The embryo therefore becomes a human being in the womb from the moment that its form is completed [i.e., at conception–DM]. The law of Moses, indeed, punishes with due penalties the man who shall cause abortion, inasmuch as there exists already the rudiment of a human being, which has imputed to it even now the condition of life and death (1973, 3:217-218).

So Exodus 21 envisioned a situation in which two brawling men accidentally injure a pregnant bystander. The injury causes the woman to go into early labor, resulting in a premature birth of her child. If neither the woman nor the child is harmed, then the Law of Moses levied a fine against the one who caused the premature birth. But if injury or even death resulted from the brawl, then the law imposed a parallel punishment: if the premature baby died, the one who caused the premature birth was to be executed–life for life. To cause a pre-born infant's death was homicide under the Old Testament–homicide punishable by death.

Notice that this Mosaic regulation had to do with injury inflicted indirectly and **accidentally**: "The phrasing of the case suggests that we are dealing with an instance of unintentional battery involving culpability" (Fishbane, p. 92). Abortion, on the other hand, is a **deliberate**, **purposeful, intentional** termination of a child's life. If God dealt severely with the **accidental** death of a pre-born infant, how do you suppose He feels about the **deliberate** murder of the unborn by an abortion doctor in collusion with the mother? The Bible states explicitly how He feels: "[D]o not kill the innocent and righteous. For I will not justify the wicked" (Exodus 23:7). As a matter of fact, one of the things that God **hates** is "hands that shed innocent blood" (Proverbs 6:17). One is reminded of moments in history when invading armies inflicted horrible atrocities on their victims, including ripping open pregnant women (2 Kings 8:12; 15:16; Hosea 13:16; Amos 1:13). Abortion is a serious matter with God. We absolutely must base our views on **God's** will—not the will of men. The very heart and soul of this great nation is being ripped out by unethical actions like abortion. We must return to the Bible as our standard of behavior—before it is too late.

When one contemplates the passages examined above in light of what is happening in society, one surely is dumbfounded. For example, women have been indicted and convicted of the murder of their own children—children who were just born and abandoned (e.g., LaRue, 2003). The news media nationwide, and society in general, have been up in arms and outraged at the unconscionable behavior of mothers who have so harmed their young children as to result in death (e.g., "Texas Mother...," 2001). Most Americans have been incensed that a mother could have so little regard for her own offspring. Yet the **same** society and the **same** news media that are outraged at such behavior would have been perfectly content for the **same** mother to murder the **same** children if she had simply chosen to do so **a few minutes or a few months before those children actually came from her womb!** Such is the insanity of a civilization that has become estranged from God—a society that places sex above sanity.

BABIES, EAGLES, AND THE RIGHT TO LIVE

Ironically, the foundational principles of the American way of life, articulated by the Founding Fathers and subsequent spokesmen, speak to this matter. The *Declaration of Independence* boldly declares: "We hold these truths to be self-evident; that all men are created equal, and that they are endowed by their Creator with certain unalienable rights; that among these are **life**, liberty, and the pursuit of happiness" (emp. added). The United States *Constitution* announced: "We the people of the United States, in order to form a more perfect union, establish justice, insure domestic tranquility, provide for the common defense, promote the general welfare, and secure the blessings of liberty to ourselves and our **posterity**, do ordain and establish this constitution for the United States of America" (emp. added). The fifth amendment of the *Constitution* in the Bill of Rights states: "Nor shall any person...be **deprived of life**, liberty, or property without due process of law" (emp. added). And Abraham Lincoln, in his *Gettysburg Address*, reminded his audience: "Four score and seven years ago, our forefathers brought forth on this continent a new nation, conceived in liberty, and dedicated to the proposition that **all men are created equal**" (emp. added).

Yet, abortion advocates subtly shift attention away from the **living** status of the unborn to the "rights" and "choice" of the mother. Abortionists style themselves "pro-choice." The hypocrisy and utter self-contradiction of such thinking is evident in their equally passionate stance on "animal rights." Millions of dollars have been spent in recent years in attempts to "save the whales." A "ruckus" has frequently arisen over the plight of endangered animal species, from the spotted owl and the dolphin, to the Snail Darter in the Little Tennessee River. One electric power provider in Utah and Colorado was fined $100,000, given three years probation, and ordered to retrofit its utility lines due to the occasional electrocution of protected bird species by its electric lines and equipment.

The Bald and Golden Eagle Protection Act provides for the protection of two species of eagles by prohibiting the taking, possession, sale, purchase, barter, offer to sell, transport, export or import, of either eagle, alive or dead, including any part, nest, or egg without a permit. "Take" means to pursue, shoot, shoot at, poison, wound, kill, capture, trap, collect, molest, or disturb. Felony convictions for the violation of this act carry a maximum fine of $250,000 or two years of imprisonment (or five years under the Lacey Act; "Bald Eagle," 2002). Get this: A human being may be fined **a quarter of a million dollars** and **put in prison for five years** for **collecting** eagle eggs, but that same person is permitted by federal law to **murder** an unborn human infant! Eagle eggs, i.e., **pre-born eagles**, are of greater value to society than **pre-born humans**! What more terrible, tragic inconsistency and incongruity could possibly exist in this country? Merely **taking possession** of an egg containing the pre-born American bald eagle—let alone if one were to destroy that little pre-birth environment and thus destroy the eagle that is developing within—results in a stiff fine and even prison time. Yet one can take a **human child** in its pre-born environment and **murder** that child—with the blessing and funding of the government!

If the right to life applies to birds, fish, and mammals—whether in pre-birth or post-birth form—how in the world can anyone arrive at the conclusion that pre-born human infants are any **less** deserving of protection? What person, in their right mind, would assign more objective worth to an **animal** than to a **human**? The abandonment of sense and sanity in assessing God's Creation, with His endowment of humans with qualities that set them miles apart from animals, has led to the nonsensical, utterly irrational thinking that presently permeates civilization. The widespread societal sanction of abortion, along with other morally objectionable behaviors like illicit drug use, gambling, and the consumption of alcohol, have together gradually and insidiously chipped away at the moral foundations of America. In the words of former United States Court of Appeals judge, Robert Bork: "The systematic killing of unborn children in huge numbers is part of a general disregard for human life…. Abortion has **coarsened** us" (1996, p. 192, emp. added).

To view the preservation of **animal** life as **equally** important—let alone **more** important—than the preservation of **human** life is a viewpoint that is seismic in its proportions and nightmarish in its implications. Whatever one's stance may be with regard to the environment and animal life, the blurring of the distinction between man and animal–so characteristic of the atheistic, humanistic, and hedonistic perspective throughout human history–inevitably contributes to moral decline, ethical desensitization, and the overall cheapening of the sanctity of human life. Instead of fretting over the potential loss of an alleged cure for AIDS or cancer due to the destruction of the rain forests, we would do well to spend that time weeping and mourning over the loss of millions of babies whose unrealized and incomprehensible potential for good has been forever expunged by abortion. The remarkably resourceful potential of those extinguished tiny human minds to have one day found a cure for cancer far surpasses the value of moss and fungi in some Third World rain forest.

The ethical disharmony and moral confusion that reign in our society have escalated the activity of criminals who commit a variety of heinous crimes. In fact, crime in the United States accounts for more death, injuries, and loss of property then all natural disasters combined (*United States...*, 2000). Yet, a sizeable portion of society opposes capital punishment. Many people feel that these lawless adults, who have engaged in heinous, destructive conduct, should not be executed–a viewpoint that flies directly in the face of what the Bible teaches (Romans 13:1-6; 1 Peter 2:13-14). God wants evildoers in society to be punished, even to the point of capital punishment–a fact recognized by the Founding Fathers when, on December 15, 1791, they ratified the Fifth Amendment of the *Constitution* (see "The U.S. Constitution..."). Yet, some absolutely refuse to execute guilty, hardened criminals, but fully endorse the execution of innocent human babies! In the name of humanity, how can anyone embrace this terrible disparity and the horrible scourge of abortion?

It is absolutely imperative that people view reality from the perspective of the Supreme, Transcendent Ruler of the Universe. As Creator, He alone is in the position to define the value of human life. God is spirit (John 4:24). He created humans in His image (Genesis 1:26). Humans are not animals. Each human possesses a soul—a spirit (Ecclesiastes 3:21). An animal does not. Unborn babies possess a spirit, and are regarded by God as human (Psalm 139:13-16; Jeremiah 1:5; Luke 1:44). How dare we regard them any differently? We should be concerned about our environment. We should give a proper measure of care and concern to the animal population. God cares and provides for His nonhuman creatures (Job 38:41; Psalm 147:9; Matthew 10:29). However, in contemplating the "birds of the air" (which certainly includes the bald eagle and the spotted owl), Jesus' own assessment of the situation is sobering, authoritative, and decisive: **"[H]ow much more valuable you are than birds!"** (Luke 12:24, NIV, emp. added; cf. Matthew 6:26; 10:31).

The ultimate solution to every moral issue is genuine New Testament Christianity and the objective standard of the Bible. If all people would organize their lives around the precepts and principles presented in the Bible, Western civilization could secure its future. No other suitable alternative exists. There is simply no other way to live life cohesively, with focus, with perspective, with direction, and with the proper sense of the purpose of life.

President Ronald Reagan wrote definitively regarding abortion—a fitting conclusion to this chapter:

> Abortion concerns not just the unborn child, it concerns every one of us. The English poet, John Donne, wrote: "...any man's death diminishes me, because I am involved in mankind; and therefore never send to know for whom the bell tolls; it tolls for thee." We cannot diminish the value of one category of human life—the unborn—without diminishing the value of all human life (1984, p. 18).

CHAPTER FOUR

THE HORROR OF HOMOSEXUALITY

Monday, May 17, 2004, was a day that will live in moral and spiritual infamy. Homosexual and lesbian couples were granted by the state of Massachusetts the right to marry—the first state in U.S. history to do so. On November 18, 2003, four activist justices of the Massachusetts Supreme Court paved the way for this occurrence by ruling that the Commonwealth must recognize the right of homosexual couples to marry ("Is Homosexual Marriage…?," 2003). Perhaps this should not be surprising, since only five months earlier, the U.S. Supreme Court issued its historically and constitutionally unprecedented elimination of State sodomy laws (*Lawrence…*, 2003)—a reversal of the high court's own 1986 decision that upheld State sodomy laws and reinforced the historic stance that homosexuality is not a constitutional right (*Bowers v. Hardwick*, 1986).

These events were the culmination of four decades of "political correctness" orchestrated by social engineers who have steadily chipped away at the "moral majority" to achieve their agenda. Though women have always been the guardians, the bastions, the last line of defense, in protecting society's sexual and moral purity, the feminist movement of the 1960s has been a significant contributor to the advancement of the homosexual agenda (cf. Bork, 1996, p. 197). The public school system has also been a co-conspirator in the effort to subvert an entire generation of children by breaking down societal sensibilities with books like *Heather Has Two Mommies* and *Daddy's Roommate*. Large corporations implemented "sensitivity training" to bully their employees into silence as more and more homosexuals boldly "came out of the closet." A change in vocabulary was quickly adopted. Homosexuality ceased being referred to as **sodomy**– the longtime historical term for same-sex relations. Now, homosexuals are referred to as "gay," and their sexual immorality is billed as an "alternative lifestyle."

As a result of the changing social norms of the baby-boomer generation in the 1960s and the pressure of an emerging politically active "gay" community, the American Psychiatric Association deleted homosexuality from its official nomenclature of mental disorders, the *Diagnostic and Statistical Manual of Mental Disorders,* in 1973 (see *American Psychiatric...*, 2002). The American Psychological Association followed suit in 1975 (Herek, 2002). Thereafter, every major mental health organization in the country quickly fell into line with the Gestapo-like tactics of those who castigated anyone who dared to disagree as "homophobes," "hatemongers," "bigots," "puritanical fanatics," and "religious fundamentalists." Indeed, those who disapprove of the homosexual "lifestyle" are declared guilty of the unpardonable sin– the sin of **intolerance** (see Bloom, 1987, p. 25).

The homosexual movement has achieved its first objective. It has been successful in reversing the historically universal rejection by American civilization of the legality, political legitimacy, and social propriety of homosexuality. The second objective is now swiftly approaching: to criminalize all **verbal** opposition to homosexuality as "hate speech" (e.g., "Bible as Hate Speech...," 2004; "Bible Verses Regarded...," 2003). One of the central means for achieving these objectives–"free speech"–is now being conveniently brushed aside in order to silence opposition!

THE FOUNDERS

These defiant overtures fly in the face of those who were responsible for creating this nation and its laws. Indeed, the Founding Fathers of these United States would be incredulous, incensed, and outraged. They understood that the acceptance of homosexuality would undermine and erode the moral foundations of civilization. Sodomy, in fact, was treated as criminal behavior in **all of the original thirteen colonies/states** and eventually every one of the fifty states (see Robinson, 2003; "Sodomy Laws...," 2003). In 1986, the U.S. Supreme Court acknowledged this longstanding fact throughout the history of Western civilization: "Proscriptions against that conduct have ancient roots.... Sodomy was a criminal offense at common law and was forbidden by the laws of the original 13 States when they ratified the Bill of Rights" (see *Bowers v. Hardwick,* 1986).

Indeed, severe penalties were invoked on those who engaged in homosexuality. Few Americans are even aware that the penalty for homosexuality in four states (New York, Vermont, Connecticut, and South Carolina) was **death** (Barton, 2000, pp. 306, 482). The other states had harsh penalties, including imprisonment for life at hard labor. Most people nowadays would be shocked to learn that **Thomas Jefferson advocated dismemberment** as the penalty for homosexuality in his home state of Virginia, and even authored a bill to that effect (1903-1904, 1: 226-227).

Where did the Founding Fathers and early American citizenry derive their views on homosexuality? Ultimately, the historically unequivocal answer is–the Bible. The Founders were influenced by the great British legal scholar, Sir William Blackstone, whose *Commentaries on the Laws of England* (1765-1769) formed the foundation for America's legal system. However, he, too, was simply echoing the biblical position. Read carefully from his Book IV (dealing with "Public Wrongs"), Chapter 15 ("Of Offenses Against the Persons of Individuals"), Section 4:

> IV. What has been here observed, especially with regard to the manner of proof, which ought to be the more clear in proportion as the crime is the more detestable, may be applied to another offense, of a still deeper malignity; **the infamous crime against nature, committed either with man or beast.** A crime, which ought to

be strictly and impartially proved, and then as strictly and impartially punished. But it is **an offense of so dark a nature**, so easily charged, and the negative so difficult to be proved, that the accusation should be clearly made out: for, if false, it deserves a punishment inferior only to that of the crime itself.

I Will not act so disagreeable part, to my readers as well as myself, as to dwell any longer upon a subject, **the very mention of which is a disgrace to human nature**. It will be more eligible to imitate in this respect the delicacy of our English law, which treats it, in its very indictments, as **a crime not fit to be named**; "*peccatum illud horribile, inter Christianos non nominandum*" ["that horrible sin, not to be named among Christians"–DM]. A taciturnity observed likewise by the edict of Constantius and Constans: "*ubi scelus est id, quod non proficit scire, jubemus infurgere leges, armari jura gladio ultore, ut exquisitis poenis subdantur insames, qui funt, vel qui futuri funt, rei*" ["When that crime is found, which is not profitable to know, we order the law to bring forth, to provide justice by force of arms with an avenging sword, that the infamous men be subjected to the due punishment, those who are found, or those who future will be found, in the deed"–DM]. Which leads me to add a word concerning its punishment.

This the voice of nature and of reason, and **the express law of God**, determine to be **capital**. Of which we have a signal instance, long before the Jewish dispensation, by the destruction of two cities by fire from heaven: so that this is an universal, not merely a provincial, precept. And our ancient law in some degree imitated this punishment, by commanding such miscreants to be burnt to death; though Fleta says they should be buried alive: either of which punishments was indifferently used for this crime among the ancient Goths. But now the general punishment of all felonies is the same, namely, by **hanging**: and this offense (being in the times of popery only subject to ecclesiastical censures) was made single felony by the statute 25 Hen. VIII. c. 6. and felony without benefit of clergy by statute 5 Eliz. c. 17. And the rule of law herein is, that, if both are arrived at years of discretion, *agentes et* *consentientes pari poena plectantur* ["advocates and con-spirators should be punished with like punishment" – DM] (1765-1769, emp. added). This stance was the very viewpoint held by the Founders and the citizenry of the entire nation from day one. "Traditional" (i.e., biblical) marriage in this country has always been between a man and a woman. No wonder the highest court in the land re-affirmed the consistent stance of 200+ years in its 1986 ruling when the Supreme Court justices declared: "The Constitution does not confer a fundamental right upon homosexuals to en-gage in sodomy" (*Bowers v. Hardwick*). In the words of Chief Jus-tice Warren Burger's concurring opinion: "[I]n constitutional terms there is no such thing as a fundamental right to commit homosexual sodomy" (*Bowers v. Hardwick*).

WHAT THE BIBLE SAYS

In the midst of this reshaping of societal sensibilities, some who wish to retain their affiliation with the Bible, yet also main-tain political correctness, insist that the Bible itself teaches that same-sex relations are not inherently sinful. They argue that the Bible, in fact, **condones** homosexuality in the same way and to the same extent that it approves of heterosexuality. But may this viewpoint be sustained biblically? What, precisely, is God's will concerning human sexuality?

Homosexuality in the Patriarchal Period

That will was demonstrated originally in the creation of the first human beings: "So God created man in His own image; in the image of God He created him; **male and female** He created them" (Genesis 1:27, emp. added). God's decision to create a fe-male counterpart to the male was not coincidental. The female uniquely met three essential criteria: (1) "It is not good for man to be alone" (Genesis 2:18); (2) a helper **suitable** to him was needed (Genesis 2:18,20); and (3) the human race was to be per-petuated through sexual union (Genesis 1:28). Both Jesus and Paul reiterated this same understanding (Matthew 19:4-6; 1 Corinthians 7:2). So the woman was: (a) the divine antidote to Adam's loneliness; (b) a helper **fit** and comparable for him; and (c) the appropriate partner for achieving the propagation of the human race.

Observe that the male and female anatomies as created by God at the beginning were designed to complement each other in terms of sexual union. They were **designed** for sexual intimacy! Here we see the divine arrangement for the human species. Theoretically, God could have created two males who had the power to unite sexually to produce offspring. Or perhaps He could have done the same with two females. Or perhaps God could have avoided creating gender distinctions at all. But His divine will is manifested in what He did: "male and female He created them" (Genesis 1:27). Here is the **natural** arrangement as established by the Creator Himself.

Not long after God set into motion the created order–which He had pronounced as "very good" (Genesis 1:31)–man began to tamper with the divine will, and altered God's original intentions concerning human sexuality. Lamech–not God–introduced polygamy into the world (Genesis 4:19). God could have created two or more women for Adam, but He did not. Rather, He made **one man for one woman for life**. That is the divine will–"Therefore **a man** [male–DM] shall leave his father [a male–DM] and mother [a female–DM] and be joined to **his wife** [female–DM], and they shall become one flesh" (Genesis 2:24, emp. added). Notice: a single man for a single woman. Genesis 19 now comes into view:

> Now the two angels came to Sodom in the evening, and Lot was sitting in the gate of Sodom. When Lot saw them, he rose to meet them, and he bowed himself with his face toward the ground. And he said, "Here now, my lords, please turn in to your servant's house and spend the night, and wash your feet; then you may rise early and go on your way," And they said, "No, but we will spend the night in the open square." But he insisted strongly; so they turned in to him and entered his house.

> Then he made them a feast, and baked unleavened bread, and they ate. Now before they lay down, the men of the city, the men of Sodom, both young and old, all the people from every quarter, surrounded the house. And they called to Lot and said to him, "Where are the men who came to you tonight? Bring them out to us that we may know them carnally." So Lot went out to them through the doorway, shut the door behind him, and said, "Please, my brethren, do not do so wickedly! See now, I have two daughters who have not known a man; please, let me bring them out to you, and you may do to them as you wish; only do nothing to these men, since this is the reason they have come under the shadow of my roof." And they said, "Stand back!" Then they said, "This one came in to sojourn, and he keeps acting as a judge; now we will deal worse with you than with them." So they pressed hard against the man Lot, and came near to break down the door. But the men reached out their hands and pulled Lot into the house with them, and shut the door. And they struck the men who were at the doorway of the house with blindness, both small and great, so that they became weary trying to find the door (Genesis 19:1-11, NKJV).

Defenders of homosexuality who seek justification for their viewpoint from the Bible have pursued a revisionist interpretation of the account of the destruction of the cities of Sodom and Gomorrah (along with Admah and Zeboim, Deuteronomy 29: 23). This passage has traditionally been understood to be a denunciation of homosexuality. This understanding has been so universal that the word "sodomy" was incorporated into English vernacular as referring to "any of various forms of sexual intercourse held to be unnatural or abnormal, especially anal intercourse or bestiality" (*American Heritage Dictionary of the English Language*, 2000, p. 1651). How may the Sodom account be reinterpreted to place same-sex relations in a favorable light? Two explanations have been offered in an effort to salvage a claim to biblical legitimacy for homosexuality.

Inhospitality or Homosexuality?

The first claim maintains that the men of Sodom were simply guilty of inhospitality. The text says that the men of Sodom insisted on Lot bringing the angelic visitors out to them, "that we may know them" (Genesis 19:5). It is argued that "know" refers to their intention to meet, greet, get to know, or become acquainted with the visitors. However, contextual indicators exclude the feasibility of this interpretation.

First, the Hebrew verb translated "know" (*yada*) certainly has a wide range of meanings, including "to get to know, to become acquainted." For the most part, the nuances of the Hebrew verb parallel the corresponding English verb. However, Hebrew, in common with other ancient languages, also used "know" as a euphemism for sexual intercourse (Genesis 4:1; 19:8). Other semitic euphemisms similarly used include "lie with" (2 Samuel 11:4), "uncover the nakedness of" (Leviticus 18), "go in unto" (Genesis 16:2; 38:2), and "touch" (Genesis 20:6; Proverbs 6:29; 1 Corinthians 7:1). Ancient languages that shared this figurative use of "know" included Egyptian (Bergman, 1986, 5:454-455), Akkadian, and Ugaritic (Botterweck, 1986, 5:456,460) as well as Syriac, Arabic, Ethiopic, and Greek (Gesenius, 1847, p. 334). When Hebrew scholars define "know" as used in Genesis 19:5, they use terminology like "sexual perversion" (Harris, et al., 1980, p. 366), "homosexual intercourse" (Botterweck, 5:464), and "crimes against nature" (Gesenius, p. 334).

Second, if "know" simply means "to get acquainted," why does the Bible repeatedly use forms of the word "wicked" to refer to the actions of the Sodomites? Lot pleaded, "Do not do so wickedly!" (Genesis 19:7). Moses, by inspiration, had already given God's assessment in the words, "But the men of Sodom were exceedingly wicked and sinful against the Lord" (Genesis 13:13); "their sin is very grievous" (Genesis 18:20). Peter referred to the "filthy conduct of the wicked" and their "lawless deeds" (2 Peter 2:7-8). But "getting acquainted" is not "wicked"! In fact, if the men of Sodom were nothing more than a group of friendly civic-minded neighbors who sought to make the visitors welcome to their city, God surely would have **commended** them—not **condemned** them!

Third, if "know" simply means "to get to know," why did Lot offer his daughters to the men? He would not have offered his daughters for the purpose of the men "getting to know" or "becoming acquainted" with them. The daughters were already residents of Sodom and would have been known to the men. Lot was offering his daughters to the men as **sexual alternatives**. Lot said, "I have two daughters **who have not known a man**" (Genesis 19:8, emp. added). "Known" is another reference to sexual intercourse. Lot referred to their sexual status for the very reason that these men were interested in sexual impropriety. As astonishing and objectionable to us as it may seem for a father to sacrifice his own daughters in such a fashion, it verifies the fact that the unnatural lust of homosexuality was considered far more repugnant than even illicit heterosexuality. Scholars have further noted that in antiquity, a host was to protect his guests at the cost of his own life (Whitelaw, 1950, 1:253).

Fourth, the men of Sodom threatened Lot with the words, "we will deal worse with you than with them" (Genesis 19:9). If their intention was simply to "get to know" the visitors, what would "dealing worse" with Lot entail? Perhaps it would have entailed becoming so thoroughly "acquainted" with Lot that they would perpetually remain in his presence and make a pest of themselves? Maybe they intended to impose on Lot's hospitality to the point that they would monopolize his living room couch, consume his snack foods, and refuse to vacate his home at a courteous hour?

In a further effort to achieve sanction for homosexuality, attention has been directed to the words of Jesus in His commissioning of the Seventy. He instructed them, in their evangelistic travels, to enter into those cities that would receive them and feel free to partake of their hospitality (Luke 10:7-8). However, should a city fail to receive them, they were to shake the dust off their feet against the city (Luke 10:10-11). Jesus then declared, "It will be more tolerable in that Day for Sodom than for that city" (Luke 10:12). Defenders and practitioners of same-sex relations claim that Jesus was drawing a comparison between the inhospitality of Sodom and the cities that the disciples would encounter. They claim that the inhospitality of a city that would reject Christ's own emissaries would be a greater evil than Sodom's inhospitable treatment of the angelic visitors.

However, if "hospitality" was the issue at stake in Sodom, the Sodomites should have been commended since they only wanted to "get to know" and be hospitable to the visitors. In fact, Lot should have been the one condemned, since he attempted to deter the hospitable overtures of the "Welcome Wagon." In reality, the words of Jesus in Luke 10 were not directed against the cities' refusal to be hospitable toward the disciples. Rather, He condemned them for their refusal to accept the teaching of the disciples. Jesus pinpointed their task when He warned: "He who hears you hears Me, he who rejects you rejects Me" (Luke 10: 16). Jesus placed Sodom at the top of the list of the most notoriously wicked cities of antiquity. He stressed the fact that, to reject Christ and the Gospel would be a far greater offense than what the most wicked city in human history ever did. What the inhabitants of Sodom did was repulsive, repugnant, disgusting, and incredibly depraved. But to reject the antidote to sin is the **ultimate** insult and the final infraction against God.

Yet another argument marshaled in an effort to justify homosexuality concerns the allusions in the prophets to Sodom. Isaiah (3:9), Jeremiah (23:14), and Ezekiel (16:49) all refer to the sinfulness of Sodom, but none explicitly mentioned homosexuality as the problem. In fact, Ezekiel pinpointed the specific sins of "pride, fullness of food, and abundance of idleness," as well as her unwillingness to aid the poor and needy. In response, we should not be surprised that a city that was guilty of sexual perversion would also be guilty of additional violations of God's will.

Isaiah, in his discussion of Sodom, did not specify a particular sin, but merely noted how brazen and open the Sodomites were with their sin: "The look on their countenance witnesses against them, and they declare their sin as Sodom; they do not hide it." Interestingly, this depiction is very apropos of the "in your face" attitude of those who seek to advance the homosexual agenda in our day. Jeremiah made essentially the same point in his comparison between Judah and Sodom when he wrote: "no one turns back from his wickedness." He, too, was noting the Sodomites' blatant, unbending, determined intention to proceed with their sin. Ezekiel, though mentioning the additional sins listed above, nevertheless referred repeatedly to Sodom's "abomination" (16: 50; cf. vss. 43,47,51,52,58). Moses linked "abomination" with homosexual activity (Leviticus 18:22).

Homosexual Rape?

The second explanation offered to justify homosexual relations is that the men of Sodom were not condemned for their homosexuality, but for their inhospitable intention to engage in homosexual **rape**. Rape, some suggest (whether homosexual or heterosexual), being nonconsensual, is wrong and worthy of condemnation. However, this extension of the inhospitality quibble is likewise contextually indefensible. First, if gang rape was the issue, why did Lot offer his daughters in exchange for the visitors? Rape would have been at stake in both cases. Lot's offer of his daughters indicated his concern over gender and same-sex relations. Second, the men of Sodom were declared wicked and guilty of "very grievous" sin before the visitors ever came to town (Genesis 18:20).

Third, Jude cinched the matter in his allusion to the sin of Sodom. He said that Sodom and her sister cities had "given themselves over to sexual immorality and gone after strange flesh" (Jude 7). "Given themselves over to sexual immorality" is a translation of the compound word *ekporneusasai* which combines the verb *porneuo* (to commit illicit sexual intercourse) with the preposition *ek* (out of). The attachment of the prepositional prefix indicates intensification, i.e., that the men of Sodom possessed "a lust that gluts itself" (Thayer, 1901, p. 199). Their sexual appetites took them beyond the range of normal sexual activity. The idea of force or coercion is not in the meaning of the word. Summarizing, Jude asserted that the sin of Sodom was homosexual **relations**–not homosexual **rape**.

Fourth, homosexuality itself is specifically condemned in Scripture. Under the Law of Moses, God made homosexuality a capital crime, and stipulated that **both** participants in the illicit sexual activity were to be put to death (Leviticus 20:13). God would not have required the innocent victim of homosexual rape to be executed along with the rapist.

Angel Flesh?

Before leaving the case of Sodom and Gomorrah, additional comments are in order in view of the remarks of Jude. Some defenders of homosexuality maintain that Jude condemned the men of Sodom–not for their homosexuality–but because they sought to have sexual relations with angels. They base this claim on the use of the expression "strange flesh": "as Sodom and Gomorrah, and the cities around them in a similar manner to these, having given themselves over to sexual immorality and **gone after strange flesh**, are set forth as an example, suffering the vengeance of eternal fire" (Jude 7, emp. added). The reasoning is that the men of Sodom were guilty of desiring sexual relations with the angelic visitors (Genesis 19:1-5). However, several problems are inherent in this interpretation.

The Meaning of "Strange"

In the first place, the English word "strange" (KJV, NKJV, ASV, NASB) creates a different meaning in the mind of the English reader than what is intended by the Greek word *heteros.* The term simply means "other, another" (Beyer, 1964, 2:702-704). Moulton and Milligan note "how readily *heteros* from meaning 'the other class (of two)' came to imply 'different' in quality or kind" (1930, p. 257; cf. Arndt and Gingrich, 1957, p. 315). Thayer even defined the word as "one not of the same nature, form, class, kind," giving Jude 7 as an instance of this use (1901, p. 254). However, he did not intend by this definition to imply that the difference extended to **angelic** flesh, as is evident from his treatment of the

THE HORROR OF HOMOSEXUALITY

verse in his section dealing with *sarx* (flesh): "to follow after the flesh, is used of those who are on the search for persons with whom they can gratify their lust, Jude 7" (p. 570; cf. p. 449). In their handling of either "strange" or "flesh," none of these lexicographers offers any support for the connotation of nonhuman or extraterrestrial, i.e., angelic.

It so happens that eminent Greek scholar A.T. Robertson disputes even the idea that the meaning of *heteros* extends to the notion of "different." In his massive and monumental *A Grammar of the Greek New Testament*, Robertson made the following comment on this term:

> The sense of "different" grows naturally out of the notion of duality. The two things **happen just to be** different.... **The word itself does not mean "different,"** but merely "one other," a second of two. It does not necessarily involve "the secondary idea of difference of kind" (Thayer). That is only true where the context demands it (1934, p. 748, emp. added).

So the notion of a different nature, form, or kind does not inhere in the word itself. Only contextual indicators can indicate, quite coincidentally, that the "other" being referred to also is different in some additional quality.

Many English translations of Jude 7 more accurately reflect the meaning of *heteros* by avoiding the use of the term "strange." For example, the RSV renders the phrase in question as "indulged in unnatural lust." The NIV and TEV read: "sexual immorality and perversion." Moffatt's translation reads: "vice and sensual perversity." Goodspeed, Beck, Weymouth, and the Twentieth Century New Testament all have "unnatural vice." The Simplified New Testament has "homosexuality." The Jerusalem Bible reads: "The fornication of Sodom and Gomorrah and the other nearby towns was equally unnatural." Even the Living Bible Paraphrased suitably pinpoints the import of the original in the words, "And don't forget the cities of Sodom and Gomorrah and their neighboring towns, all full of lust of every kind, **including lust of men for other men.**"

Considering the meaning of "strange" in its only occurrences (in English) in the KJV (11 times), NKJV (7 times), ASV (10 times), RSV (6 times), and NIV (5 times), one finds that it never is used to refer to angels, but instead refers to: "strange things" (Luke 5: 26–i.e., a miracle); "strange land" (Acts 7:6–i.e., Egypt); "strange gods" (Acts 17:18); "strange things" (Acts 17:20–i.e., ideas); "strange cities" (Acts 26:11–i.e., Gentile or outside Palestine); "strange tongues" (1 Corinthians 14:21–i.e., foreign languages); "strange country" (Hebrews 11:9–i.e., Canaan); "strange doctrines" (Hebrews 13:9); "think it strange" (1 Peter 4:4–i.e., odd); "some strange thing" (1 Peter 4:12–i.e., unusual); and "strange flesh" (Jude 7–i.e., male with male). All the other occurrences of the underlying Greek term in the New Testament further undergird the nonapplication of the term to "angelic flesh" (Moulton, et al., 1978, pp. 392-393).

Most commentators and language scholars recognize this feature of Jude's remark, as evinced by their treatment of Jude 7. For example, the *New Analytical Greek Lexicon* defines *heteros* in Jude 7 as "illicit" (Perschbacher, 1990, p. 177). Williams identifies "strange flesh" as "unnatural vice" (1960, p. 1023). Barclay wrote: "What the men of Sodom were bent on was unnatural sexual intercourse, homosexual intercourse, with Lot's two visitors. They were bent on sodomy, the word in which their sin is dreadfully commemorated" (1958, p. 218). Alford correctly translated the Greek as "other flesh," and defined the phrase as "[other] than that appointed by God for the fulfillment of natural desire" (1875, 4: 533). Jamieson, et al., define "going after strange flesh" as "departing from the course of nature, and going after that which is unnatural" (n.d., p. 544). Schneider says the expression "denotes licentious living" (1964, 2:676; cf. Hauck, 1967, 4:646; Seesemann, 1967, 5:292). Macknight said: "They committed the unnatural crime which hath taken its name from them" (n.d., p. 693). Mayor explained, "the forbidden flesh (literally 'other than that appointed by God') refers...in the case of Sodom to the departure from the natural use" (n.d., 5:260). Barnes states: "the word *strange*, or *other*, refers to that which is contrary to nature"

(1978, p. 392, italics in orig.), and Salmond adds, "a departure from the laws of nature in the impurities practiced" (1950, p. 7).

The frequent allusion to "nature" and "unnatural" by scholars must not be taken to mean "beyond nature" in the sense of beyond human, and thereby somehow a reference to angels. The same scholars frequently clarify their meaning in unmistakable terms. For example, after defining "strange flesh" as unnatural, Jamieson, Faussett, and Brown add: "In later times the most enlightened heathen nations indulged in the sin of Sodom without compunction or shame" (n.d., p. 544). Alford, likewise, added: "The sin of Sodom was afterwards common in the most enlightened nations of antiquity" (4:533). It is neither without significance nor coincidental that these Bible scholars focus on forms of the word "natural," in view of the fact that Scripture elsewhere links same-sex relations with that which is "**against nature**" (Romans 1:26-27) or unnatural—i.e., out of harmony with the original arrangement of nature by God at the Creation (e.g., Genesis 1:27; 2:22; Matthew 19:4-6).

Contextual Indicators

In the second place, beyond the technical meanings and definitions of the words in Jude 7, contextual indicators also exclude the interpretation that the sin of the men of Sodom was not homosexuality but their desire for angelic flesh. Look again at the wording of the verse: "as Sodom and Gomorrah, **and the cities around them** in a similar manner to these...." To what cities does Jude refer? The Bible actually indicates that Sodom and Gomorrah were only two out of five wicked cities situated on the plain, the other three being Zoar, Admah, and Zeboim (Deuteronomy 29:23; Hosea 11:8). Zoar was actually spared destruction as a result of Lot's plea for a place to which he might flee (Genesis 19:18-22).

Do the advocates of homosexuality wish to hold the position that the populations of the four cities that were destroyed were **all** guilty of desiring sexual relations **with angels**? Perhaps the latest sexual fad that swept over all the cities in the vicinity was "angel sex"? And are we to believe that the great warning down through the ages regarding the infamous behavior of the inhabitants of Sodom—a warning that is repeated over and over again down through the ages to people in many places and periods of history (Deuteronomy 29:23; 32:32; Isaiah 1:9; 3:9; 13:19; Jeremiah 23:14; 49:18; 50:40; Lamentations 4:6; Ezekiel 16:46,49, 53,55; Amos 4:11; Zephaniah 2:9; Matthew 10:15; 11:24; Luke 10:12; 17:29; Romans 9:29; 2 Peter 2:6; Revelation 11:8)—is: "Do not have sex **with angels!**"? How many times have you been tempted to violate **that** warning? The opportunity presents itself on a regular basis, right? The country is full of "single angel" bars! No, what Barclay labeled as "the glare of Sodom and Gomorrah," which is "flung down the whole length of Scripture history" (p. 218), is not angel sex! It is **same**-sex relations—men with men. And, unbelievably, now the very warning that has been given down through the ages needs to be issued to America!

Additionally, the men of Sodom were already guilty of practicing homosexuality **before** the angels showed up to pronounce judgment on their behavior. That is precisely why the angels were sent to Sodom—to survey the moral landscape (Genesis 18: 21) and urge Lot and his family to flee the city (Genesis 18:23; 19:12-13,15-16). The men of Sodom were pronounced by God as "exceedingly wicked and sinful against the Lord" back at the time Lot made the decision to move to Sodom (Genesis 13:13). Lenski called attention to the Aorist participles used in Jude 7 (i.e., "having given themselves over" and "going after") as further proof of this fact: "An appeal to Gen. 19:4, etc., will not answer this question, for this occurred [i.e., the Sodomites descending on Lot's house—DM] when the cup of fornications was already full, when Jude's two aorist participles had already become facts, on the day before God's doom descended" (1966, p. 624).

One final point likewise discounts the claim that the men of Sodom were lusting after angel flesh. The men of Sodom did not know that the two individuals visiting Lot were angels. They had the **appearance** of "men" (Genesis 18:2,16,22; 19:1,5,8,10, 12,16), whose feet could be washed (Genesis 19:2) and who could consume food (Genesis 19:3). The men of Sodom could not have been guilty of desiring to have sexual relations with angels, since they could not have known the men **were** angels. Even if the men of Sodom somehow knew that the visitors were angels, the impropriety of same-sex relations remains intact–since the angels appeared in the form of **males–not females**.

An honest and objective appraisal of Jude 7 provides no support for the homosexual cause. The Bible consistently treats homosexual behavior as sinful. American culture may well reach the point where the majority approves of homosexuality as acceptable behavior. And those who disapprove may well be accused of being "politically incorrect," intolerant, and "homophobic." It surely is reminiscent of our own day to observe that when Lot urged the Sodomites not to do "so wickedly," the men accused Lot of **being judgmental** (Genesis 19:9; cf. Deuteronomy 23:17-18). Nevertheless, the objective, unbiased reader of the Bible is forced to conclude that God destroyed the men of Sodom on account of their sinful practice of homosexuality.

Homosexuality in the Mosaic Period

In addition to the pre-Mosaic, Patriarchal period of history, God made clear His will on this matter when He handed down the Law of Moses to the Israelite nation. In chapters dealing almost exclusively with sexual regulations, His words are explicit and unmistakable.

> **You shall not lie with a male as with a woman. It is an abomination**. Nor shall you mate with any beast, to defile yourself with it. Nor shall any woman stand before a beast to mate with it. It is perversion. Do not defile yourselves with any of these things; for by all these the nations are defiled, which I am casting out before you. For the land is defiled; therefore I visit the punishment of its iniquity upon it, and the land vomits out its inhabitants. You shall therefore keep My statutes and My judgments, and shall not commit any of these abominations,

either any of your own nation or any stranger who so-
journs among you (for all these abominations the men
of the land have done, who were before you, and thus
the land is defiled), lest the land vomit you out also when
you defile it, as it vomited out the nations that were before you. For whoever commits any of these abominations, the persons who commit them shall be cut off from
among their people. Therefore you shall keep My ordi-
nance, so that you do not commit any of these abominable customs which were committed before you, and that
you do not defile yourselves by them: I am the Lord your
God.... **If a man lies with a male as he lies with a
woman, both of them have committed an abomination. They shall surely be put to death**. Their blood
shall be upon them (Leviticus 18:22-30; 20:13, NKJV,
emp. added).

I suggest that a reader would need help to misunderstand these
injunctions.

Compared to Female Menstruation?

Nevertheless, attempts have been made to offset their seemingly unmistakable import. For example, it is argued that in the
same chapter (i.e., Leviticus 20), five verses after the injunction
against homosexuality, the death penalty also was required for a
man and his wife for having sexual relations during her menstruation: "If a man lies with a woman during her sickness and
uncovers her nakedness, he has exposed her flow, and she has
uncovered the flow of her blood. Both of them shall be cut off
from their people" (Leviticus 20:18). The homosexual activist
(who wishes to maintain some semblance of affiliation with the
Bible) dismisses this text as ritualistic and limited to Israel's pe-
culiar concern for purity, thus having no universal significance.
After all, so we are told, the Israelites lived during an ignorant,
primitive period of human history. Consider the following wording of this viewpoint:

Of course, many now live in quite different cultures. But
that has not stopped some from selectively using regulations like Leviticus 18:22 and 20:13 to support their con-

demnation of homosexual intimacy. Meanwhile, the Bible prohibits sex during menstruation in the very same chapters (Lev. 18:19; 20:18), but few Christian conservatives have mounted a campaign to expel people who violate that commandment (Carr, 2003).

This interpretation of the biblical position stands in conflict with several factors. First, are those who dismiss the condemnation of homosexuality, on the basis that the same context condemns sexual intimacy during a woman's menses, also willing to dismiss the condemnations in the same context of child sacrifice (20:2-5), bestiality (20:15-16), incest (20:11-12), and bigamy (20:14)? What proves too much, proves nothing.

Second, a closer reading of the text reveals that while all the items alluded to are clustered together because they share a common concern for the principle of "separateness" (which constitutes the theme of Leviticus—e.g., 10:10; 11:44; 19:2; 20:7,26), nevertheless, a distinction may be made between those actions that were temporary and limited in their scope to the Israelites and those that are clearly permanent and universal in their application. For example, child sacrifice (Leviticus 18:21; 20:2-5) has always been an abominable sin before God (cf. Deuteronomy 12:31; 18:10; 2 Kings 17:17; 2 Chronicles 28:3; 33:6; Psalm 106:37-38; Jeremiah 7:31; 19:5; 32:35; Ezekiel 23:37,39). The same may be said of bestiality (Leviticus 18:23; 20:15-16), sorcery, witchcraft, astrology, and the like (Exodus 22:18; Leviticus 19:26,31; 20:6,27; Deuteronomy 18:10-11; Isaiah 8:19; Acts 19:19), as well as various forms of incest (Leviticus 18:6-17; 20:11-12; 1 Corinthians 5:1). Homosexuality fits into this same category since it is condemned in every period of Bible history, and repeated in especially strong terms in the New Testament (Romans 1:24-27; 1 Corinthians 6:9; 1 Timothy 1:10).

This distinction is reinforced by the variations given to the penalties associated with each infraction. Two expressions must be distinguished in the pericope of Leviticus (i.e., chapters 17-20, what Pfeiffer labeled "The Holiness Code"—1957, p. 46). The first is "cut off," which, in the Pentateuch, includes being cut off "from his people," "in the sight of their people," "from among the congregation," "from Israel," "from the congregation of Israel," and "from My presence." Linguistic scholars agree that the Hebrew verb translated "cut off" (*karat*) has both a literal meaning and a metaphorical meaning, which in turn gives rise to "the extensive range of the root's literal and extended semantic spheres of meaning" (Hasel, 1995, 7:343). The basic literal meaning of the verb is "to cut" (7:344-345), and so may be used to refer to everything from cutting down a tree to cutting off a piece of cloth. However,

> In addition to the literal meaning of this root, "to cut off," ...there is the metaphorical meaning **to root out, eliminate, remove, excommunicate** or destroy by a violent act of man or nature. It is sometimes difficult in a given context to know whether the person(s) who is "cut off" is to be killed **or only excommunicated** (Harris, et al., 1980, 1:457, emp. added).

In this metaphorical sense, being "cut off" consists of "exclusion from the community" (Harris, et al., 1:457), "in the sense of being cut off from a center or circle in which the offender lives" (Hasel, 7:347).

> The "cutting off" formula therefore does not appear to refer solely to human execution of the death penalty. In the **majority** of offenses, "cutting off" means a "cutting off" which leads to **"banishment" or "excommunication"** from the cultic community and the covenant people...from life in God's presence **through exclusion** (7:348, emp. added).

Gesenius confirms this understanding of the term, recognizing that its figurative meaning is "to be cut off from one's country, i.e., to be **driven into exile**, to be **expelled**" (1847, p. 417, emp. added). Though Gesenius listed Leviticus 20:18 under the literal meaning of "to be destroyed," translator Tregelles rightfully added a note to the section: "In some of the passages it appears only to signify **severed from the congregation** of the Lord" (p. 417, emp. added).

The Scriptures themselves bear out this observation. For example, in a context addressing contact with the dead, the Israelites were told, "Whoever touches the body of anyone who has died, and does not purify himself, defiles the tabernacle of the Lord. That person shall be **cut off from Israel**. He shall be unclean, because the water of purification was not sprinkled on him; **his uncleanness is still on him**" (Numbers 19:13, emp. added; cf. vs. 20). It is evident, both from this verse and surrounding verses, that those who had been defiled by corpses were to be **separated** from the congregation for the appropriate period of purification–**not executed**.

This dual use of the expression is further confirmed by comparing it with a second one that is germane to the discussion: "put to death." Both expressions are used in Exodus 31:14–"You shall keep the Sabbath, therefore, for it is holy to you. Everyone who profanes it shall surely be **put to death**; for whoever does any work on it, that person shall be **cut off from among his people**" (emp. added). Observe that the phrase "cut off from among his people" is the broader expression. "Put to death" is the more narrow expression, and clarifies by what means the individual would be "cut off." Thus, to be "cut off" from Israel could be accomplished in two distinct and separate ways: (1) through temporary isolation of the individual by physically removing him from the community, transporting him to a location away from the social/religious life of Israel (cf. "put out of the camp"– Numbers 5:2); or (2) through permanent removal of the individual from Israelite society by legal execution, i.e., the death penalty. Context must determine which meaning is intended.

Of the twelve occurrences of *karat* ("cut off") in the Niphal conjugation of the Hebrew verb in Leviticus (see Wigram, 1890, p. 619), those outside of chapter 20 that refer to being merely quarantined for a period of time until correction/cleansing could be made, are 7:20,21,25,27; 17:4,9; 19:8; 22:3. A generic use is seen in 18:29 where it is found in a summary statement of offenses without further specification as to its meaning–since chapter 20 is intended to be the portion of the pericope that prescribes punishment for the offenses mentioned in chapter 18. The only instance in Leviticus where the expression apparently includes the death penalty is 23:29. However, even in this instance, that the death penalty is intended is derived from the verse before and the verse after, which indicate that "afflicted" (NKJV), "humble" (NASB), or "deny himself" (NIV) pertain to the defiant refusal to abstain from work on the Day of Atonement (which elsewhere was treated as a capital offense when done on a holy day—Numbers 15:33ff.), and the accompanying threat by God to "destroy" the culprit.

Additionally, when one examines the pericope with regard to prescribed penalties, those for the offenses listed in chapter 18 are not given until chapter 20 (with the exception of the generic formula, "cut off" [18:29]). Chapter 20 clarifies in what sense the offender was to be "cut off," depending upon the offense committed. "Cut off" in the Hiphil conjugation of the Hebrew verb was the penalty for child sacrifice (20:2-5), clarified as "put to death" (vs. 2), as well as for the person who engaged in sorcery, i.e., turned to mediums and spiritists (20:6), which also is further pinpointed as "put to death" (vs. 27). For adultery (20:10), certain forms of incest (20:11-12), homosexuality (20:13), and bestiality (20:15-16), the penalty was "put to death." Those who committed bigamy were to be "burned with fire" (20:14), i.e., put to death and their corpses cremated (cf. Joshua 7:15,25; Jamieson, et al., n.d., p. 88; although Clarke insisted that branding with a hot iron was meant—n.d., 1:578). For another form of incest, and relations during a woman's menstruation, only the expression "cut off" is used (20:17-18), and three other forms of incest have only "they shall bear their guilt" (20:19), "they shall die childless" (20:20), and "they shall be childless" (20:21).

When one reads all three injunctions pertaining to menstruation given in Leviticus, their meaning and harmonization become apparent:

> If a woman has a discharge, and the discharge from her body is blood, **she shall be set apart seven days**; and whoever touches her shall be unclean until evening. Ev-

erything that she lies on during her impurity shall be unclean; also everything that she sits on shall be unclean. Whoever touches her bed shall wash his clothes and bathe in water, and be unclean until evening. And whoever touches anything that she sat on shall wash his clothes and bathe in water, and be unclean until evening. If anything is on her bed or on anything on which she sits, when he touches it, he shall be unclean until evening. And **if any man lies with her at all, so that her impurity is on him, he shall be unclean seven days**; and every bed on which he lies shall be unclean (Leviticus 15:19-24, emp. added).

Also you shall not approach a woman to uncover her nakedness as long as she is in her customary impurity (Leviticus 18:19).

If a man lies with a woman during her sickness and uncovers her nakedness, he has exposed her flow, and she has uncovered the flow of her blood. **Both of them shall be cut off from their people** (Leviticus 20:18, emp. added).

Comparing the three injunctions shows that a woman was to be **set apart** from the community during her monthly menstruation. If her husband were to have sexual relations with her during that time (the implication possibly being that her menstruation commenced during intercourse, catching both unawares–see Wenham, 1979, p. 220; Keil and Delitzsch, 1976, 1:394), then he, too, was ceremonially defiled and subject to the same separation. Hence, "set apart for seven days" (15:19), "unclean seven days" (15:24), and "cut off from their people" (20:18) are three ways to express the same proscription. "Cut off" did not mean execution in this case (cf. Harris, 1990, 2:600-601).

Based upon these observations, the regulation pertaining to refraining from sexual relations during a woman's period of menstruation, when violated, did not involve the death penalty. The injunction was limited to the Israelites, and served to reinforce the concept of being a holy people. Blood, a term that is used 86 times in Leviticus, was a critical feature of this Old Testament teaching, especially in its relation to life and atonement (e.g.,

Leviticus 17:11). Beyond this central significance, the injunction could possibly have been intended to emphasize (1) the importance of being health conscious or (2) the importance of the husband being thoughtful and considerate toward his wife during a difficult time of the month.

Concerning the former, there is some debate in the medical community over whether or not intercourse during menstruation increases the risk for exposure to Pelvic Inflammatory Disease (see "Pelvic Inflammatory...," 1998; "Causes of Pelvic...," 2003; "PID," 2004). Blood, of course, can be a significant medium for bacteria and infectious diseases. As one medical authority noted: "Intercourse during menses and frequent intercourse may offer more opportunities for the admission of pathogenic organisms to the inside of the uterus" ("Pelvic Inflammatory Disease," 2001). Though great strides have been made in increasing medical understanding over the centuries, medical science has not provided all the answers to questions that still exist regarding the Bible's inspired declarations concerning various matters of health and medicine.

Concerning the latter, some authorities point out that this law was a benevolent injunction designed to render compassionate assistance to women during a difficult time (Knight, 1981, p. 83; Harris, 1990, 2:586-587,600). Even today, women are vulnerable to the whims of thoughtless men. The Law of Moses manifested a comparable concern for women in other aspects of life, including pregnancy (Exodus 21:22ff.) and unfair divorce (Deuteronomy 24:1-4). It is notable that Jesus manifested tender compassion for the poor woman who had been suffering from a hemorrhage for twelve years (Matthew 9:20ff.; Mark 5:25ff.; Luke 8:43ff.).

We are forced to conclude that some Israelite laws (like the prohibition of eating unclean foods) affected only Israel and, in most cases, were subject to penalties that simply required purification and cleansing procedures. Ulrich Falkenroth agreed: "Intercourse during menstruation...was not subject to a civil penalty but brought ritual uncleanness" (1978, 3:95). This was unquestionably the case for matters pertaining to a woman's menses. [NOTE: Interestingly, in addition to ceremonial cleansing, **both a sin and a burnt offering** were required following childbirth (Leviticus 12) and a non-menses discharge (Leviticus 15: 25-30), but not for normal monthly menstruation.] It is these very laws of ritualistic purification that are noted in the New Testament as having been confined to the Israelites prior to the cross of Christ, having no abiding relevance or application (e.g., Colossians 2:14-17; cf. Mark 7:19). On the other hand, these ceremonial laws were treated differently from the **universal** sins that repeatedly surface elsewhere in Scripture as having a broader application to all cultures in all times, i.e., lying, stealing, adultery, bestiality, child sacrifice, homosexuality, etc. Leviticus 18: 22 and 20:13 were expressions of God's will pertaining to same-sex relations that represent a **continuing prohibition** (Romans 1:24-27; 1 Corinthians 6:9; 1 Timothy 1:10; cf. Flatt, et al., 1982, pp. 27-29).

The Dark Ages

Another graphic account is presented during the period of the judges, which was a time of spiritual and moral depravity and decay—the "Dark Ages" of Jewish history. Judges 19 records that "sons of Belial" (i.e., wicked scoundrels) surrounded a house where travelers had taken refuge for the night. As in Sodom, they desired to "know" the male guest—who, by the way, was **not** an angel (vs. 22). The host, like Lot, knew exactly what they meant, as is evident from the fact that, like Lot, he offered them a sexual alternative (which, of course, God did not approve). Their sexual desire was labeled as "wickedness," "outrage," "vileness," "lewdness," and "evil" (Judges 19:23,24; 20:3,6,10,12,13, NKJV). The rest of the Old Testament corroborates this judgment of same-sex relations. For example, during the period of the kings, Josiah instituted sweeping moral and religious reforms. These included tearing down the homes of the "sodomites" (2 Kings 23:7, KJV, ASV; "perverted persons," NKJV; "male cult prostitutes," RSV, NASB).

Homosexuality in the New Testament Period

The New Testament is equally definitive in its uncompromising and unquestioned condemnation of illicit sexual activity. Paul summarized the "unrighteous" and "ungodly" behavior of the Gentile nations and declared:

> For this reason God gave them up to **vile passions**. For even their women **exchanged the natural use for what is against nature**. Likewise also the men, **leaving the natural use of the woman, burned in their lust for one another, men with men** committing what is shameful, and receiving in themselves the penalty of their error which was due. And even as they did not like to retain God in their knowledge, God gave them over to a **debased mind**, to do those things which are not fitting; being filled with all unrighteousness, **sexual immorality**, wickedness, covetousness, maliciousness; full of envy, murder, strife, deceit, evil-mindedness; they are whisperers, backbiters, haters of God, violent, proud, boasters, inventors of evil things, disobedient to parents, undiscerning, untrustworthy, unloving, unforgiving, unmerciful; who, knowing the righteous judgment of God, that **those who practice such things are worthy of death**, not only do the same but also approve of those who practice them (Romans 1:26-32, emp. added).

This passage uses Greek terms that linguistic scholars define as "forbidden desire," "impurity," "unnatural vice," "shameful passions," "not in accordance with nature," and "individuals of the same sex being inflamed with sensual, sexual desire for each other" (Arndt and Gingrich, 1957, pp. 28,118,119,240,583,877). Observe that "God gave them up" to "vile passions." Other renderings include "lusts of dishonor" (Bengel, 1971, 2:26), "passions of dishonor" (Lenski, 1951, p. 113), and "passions which bring dishonour" (Cranfield, 1985, p. 125). The passions to which the heathen nations were given are declared to be vile and debased. In fact, the "women" and "men" (i.e., the "females" and "males" of verse 26) had descended "to the brutish level of being nothing but creatures of sex" (Lenski, p. 113; Bengel, 2:26).

The contrast between the "natural" and the "unnatural" shows that the Gentiles had "left aside and thus discarded" the **natural form of intercourse between a man and his wife** (Lenski, p. 113). Paul's observation that homosexual activity goes "against nature" harks back to the Creation model when God created the first human beings (Genesis 1:26). Homosexual practices go against the natural pattern established by God when He created "male and female" (Deyoung, 1988, pp. 429-441). Such behavior is "contrary to the intention of the Creator" (Cranfield, p. 123). Therefore, homosexuality goes against the natural order of marriage among **all** nationalities and cultures.

Not only is God displeased with those who participate in homosexual behavior, but Paul indicates that He is equally displeased with those who are **supportive** of such conduct–even if they do not engage in the activity themselves. The wording is: "[T]hose who practice such things are worthy of death, not only do the same but **also approve of those who practice them**" (vs. 32). On this count alone, many have earned the disapproval of God.

In view of Corinth's notorious reputation for being dedicated to illicit sexual activity, compare Paul's remarks to the church at Rome with the question he posed to the Corinthian church:

> Do you not know that the unrighteous will not inherit the kingdom of God? Do not be deceived. Neither fornicators, nor idolaters, nor adulterers, **nor homosexuals, nor sodomites**, nor thieves, nor covetous, nor drunkards, nor revilers, nor extortioners, will inherit the kingdom of God. **And such were some of you.** But you were washed, but you were sanctified, but you were justified in the name of the Lord Jesus and by the Spirit of our God (1 Corinthians 6:9-11, emp. added).

The Greek word translated "homosexual" in this passage is a metaphorical use of a term that literally means "soft," and when referring to people, refers to males allowing themselves to be used sexually by other males. Lexicographers apply the term to the person who is a "catamite," i.e., a male who submits his body to another male for unnatural lewdness, i.e., homosexually (Thayer, 1901, p. 387; Arndt and Gingrich, 1957, p. 489).

"Sodomites" ("abusers of themselves with mankind" in the KJV) is a translation of the term *arsenokoitai*. It derives from two words: *arsein* (a male) and *koitei* (a bed), and refers to one who engages in sex with a male as with a female (Thayer, p. 75). Paul used the same term when he wrote to Timothy to discuss certain behaviors that are both "contrary to sound doctrine" and characteristic of the one who is not "a righteous man" (1 Timothy 1: 9-10). As D. Gene West correctly observed regarding Paul's letter to Timothy:

> We can see from the context that homosexual activities are classed with such sins as patricide, matricide, homicide, kidnapping, and perjury. If we accept that any of these things are sins, we must accept that all are sins. If it is a sin to be a whoremonger, to pursue a lascivious life with prostitutes, then it is likewise a sin to engage in homosexual acts. There is no way to escape that conclusion. If it is a sin to murder one's father, or mother, or some other human being, then it is a sin for both males and females to "cohabitate" (2004).

When Paul said to Christians at Corinth, "such **were** some of you," he proved not only that homosexuals may be forgiven, but that they can **cease** such sinful activity. Here we have a clear biblical indication that someone can change their sexual orientation, and be forgiven of a past immoral lifestyle. We are forced to conclude that sexual activity between persons of the same sex is **not a matter of genetics**; but is a **behavioral** phenomenon associated largely with environmental factors. This conclusion from the Bible is in complete harmony with the latest scientific evidence. The Human Genome Project was completed in 2003 (see "Human Genome Report...," 2003). The human X and Y chromosomes (the two "sex" chromosomes) were completely sequenced. Yet, neither the map for the X nor the Y chromosome contains any "gay gene." **No scientific evidence exists**

to prove a genetic basis for homosexuality (see Harrub, et al., 2004). It is not "nature," but "nurture" that is responsible. It is not a life "style," but rather a life "choice." [NOTE: Interestingly, evidence exists to show that homosexuals experience shorter life spans compared to heterosexuals (see Cameron, et al., 1993).]

CONCLUSION

Homosexuality is only one of many departures from God's will for human morality and sexuality that society is facing. The Greek word for fornication, *porneia*, is a broad term that covers **every form of illicit sexual intercourse**, including adultery, incest, bestiality, bigamy, polygamy, bisexuality, homosexuality, pedophilia, necrophilia, and more. The overall thrust of the Bible from beginning to end is one of condemnation of all such behaviors. The Bible, in fact, has more to say about homosexuality than it does the Lord's Supper!

Please understand: God loves **all** sinners—regardless of the specific sins they have committed. But it is imperative that we be about the business of alerting those who are engaged in sexual sin regarding God's will, in an effort to "snatch them out of the fire" (Jude 23), and to "save a soul from death and cover a multitude of sins" (James 5:20). One day it will be too late for both those who "not only do the same but also approve of those who practice them" (Romans 1:32). Indeed, the "sexually immoral...shall have their part in the lake which burns with fire and brimstone" (Revelation 21:8).

Sexual sin undoubtedly will go down in history as one of the major contributors to the moral and spiritual deterioration, decline, and downfall of American society. Homosexuality is one more glaring proof of the **sexual anarchy** that prevails in American civilization. One wonders how much longer such widespread unchastity can continue in our land before God will "visit the punishment of its iniquity upon it, and the land vomits out its inhabitants" (Leviticus 18:25). When professors at a **Christian** university denounce a colleague for speaking out against homosexuality, describing his remarks as "intemperate," and apologizing lest he "insulted," "demeaned," or "injured" those who may be "struggling with same-sex attraction," it is time for all of us to reacquaint ourselves with the God of the Bible by rereading His own remarks (see Tippens, 2000). Such academicians are under the spell of "political correctness" run amok. The very arguments that are currently made to legitimize homosexuality, or at least soften attitudes against it, could also be used to sanction bestiality, necrophilia, polygamy, bigamy, incest, and pedophilia. You watch–in time they will.

In the greater scheme of human history, as civilizations have proceeded down the usual pathway of moral deterioration and eventual demise, the acceptance of same-sex relations has typically triggered the final stages of impending social implosion. America is being brought to the very brink of moral catastrophe. It would appear that the warning issued by God to Israel regarding their own ability to sustain their national existence in the Promised Land is equally apropos for America:

> You shall not lie with a male as with a woman. It is an abomination…. Do not defile yourselves with any of these things; for by all these the nations are defiled, which I am casting out before you. For the land is defiled; therefore I visit the punishment of its iniquity upon it, and **the land vomits out its inhabitants**. You shall therefore keep My statutes and My judgments, and shall not commit any of these abominations…**lest the land vomit you out also** when you defile it, as it vomited out the nations that were before you (Leviticus 18:22-28, emp. added).

Unless something is done to stop the moral degeneration, America would do well to prepare for the inevitable Divine expulsion.

Every society in human history that has followed a course of moral and spiritual depravity has either been destroyed by God or has imploded from within. America will not be the exception. Like these previous civilized nations, our society will not be permitted to survive indefinitely into the future–unless, of course, God is prepared to apologize to Sodom and Gomorrah.

CHAPTER FIVE

THE PLAGUE OF PORNOGRAPHY

Pornography has always existed in American society. But for most of the nation's history, it was hidden, underground, and minimal. All that changed in the 1950s. That was the decade when *Playboy* magazine began to promote the "Playboy philosophy" and mainstream pornography to the American male. The "free love" generation of the 1960s then sanctioned the severance of sex from monogamy. The spread of pornography became rampant.

Here are the latest statistics (gleaned from "Pornography Statistics...," 2004; Hagelin, 2004; "Sex on TV...," 2001; "Sexuality...," 2001; "TV Sex Getting...," 2003; "New Look...," 2000; "More TV Sex," 2000; "Study Links TV...," 2004; "Mini-Britneys," 2004; Greenhouse, 2004)–**read 'em and weep**:

- Pornography revenue is larger than all combined revenues of all professional football, baseball, and basketball franchises.
- U.S. pornography revenue exceeds the combined revenues of ABC, CBS, and NBC ($6.2 billion).
- Child pornography generates $3 billion annually.
- The average age of first Internet exposure to pornography is 11 years old.
- The largest consumer of Internet pornography is the 12-17 age group.
- The percent of 15-17 year olds having multiple hardcore exposures is 80%.

- The percent of 8-16 year olds having viewed porn online is 90% (most while doing homework).
- The number of U.S. adults who regularly visit Internet pornography Web sites is 40 million.
- The number of pornographic Web sites is 4.2 million–12% of total Web sites.
- Sex is the number one topic searched on the Internet.
- Americans spend $10 billion per year on pornography.
- There are 800 million rentals each year of adult videos and DVDs.
- 11,000 adult movies are produced each year.
- 75 percent of prime time television in the 1999-2000 season included sexual content.
- The average American adolescent will view nearly 14,000 sexual references per year.
- 64 percent of all shows include sexual content, and only 15% mention waiting, protection, and consequences.
- Sexual content is featured once every four minutes on network TV, with 98% of all sexual content having no subsequent physical consequences, 85% of sexual behavior having no lasting emotional impact, and nearly 75% of the participants in sexual activity being unmarried.
- Sexual content on prime-time TV more than tripled in the past ten years.
- Teenagers who watch a lot of television with sexual content are twice as likely to engage in intercourse than are those who watch few such programs.
- Young people today are sexualized at an earlier and earlier age. Stars like Britney Spears and Christina Aguilera have long been criticized for exploiting their sexuality for profit. The next generation can already be seen emulating its older sisters–literally.
- *Playboy's* largest cable channel, *Playboy* TV, is available in 24 million of the nation's 81 million homes that receive either satellite, cable, or digital television.

The scourge of pornography has spread like a catastrophic plague across the nation–from the magazines of the 1950s to the Internet of the 21st century. Hollywood itself has been a willing

accomplice in the inundation of the American public with pornographic programming on television and at movie theaters
around the country.

WHAT THE BIBLE SAYS

God has defined for humanity the proper parameters of sex
and sexual allurement. Within a scriptural marriage relationship, the gratification of sexual desire may be satiated in a legal
and healthy manner (1 Corinthians 6:18; 7:2-5; Ephesians 5:3).
Beyond God's prescription for sexual fulfillment, at least three
principles are given in the Bible that have a direct bearing on the
propriety of pornography.

Lust

First, the Bible condemns lust (i.e., illicit desire). When David
accidentally saw Bathsheba taking a bath, he should have turned
away and put the image out of his mind. Instead, he allowed the
pornographic scene to "fester" and create within him a desire to
have sexual relations with her (2 Samuel 11:2-3). Pornography,
by definition, is designed to engender lust and to arouse sensual
appetites. It incites sexual appetites that are to be kept in check
and guided in accordance with God's directives. Many verses of
Scripture speak against lust. Peter pleaded with Christians: "Be-
loved, I beg you as sojourners and pilgrims, abstain from **fleshly
lusts** which war against the soul" (1 Peter 2:11-12, emp. added).
Paul commanded: "Let us walk properly, as in the day, not in
revelry and drunkenness, **not in lewdness and lust**, not in strife
and envy. But put on the Lord Jesus Christ, and make no provi-
sion for the flesh, **to fulfill its lusts**" (Romans 13:13-14, emp.
added). The NIV renders the last portion of the sentence: "**do
not think about how to gratify the desires**" of the flesh. Paul
also warned the young Timothy: "Flee also **youthful lusts**; but
pursue righteousness, faith, love, peace with those who call on
the Lord out of a pure heart" (2 Timothy 2:22, emp. added). He
warned young Titus: "For we ourselves were also once foolish,
disobedient, deceived, **serving various lusts and pleasures**...."
(3:3, emp. added).

The Mind

Second, the Bible is insistent that every individual has the responsibility to control his or her mind and avoid exposing the mind to influences that are evil or spiritually damaging. Solomon insisted: "**Keep your heart** with all diligence, for out of it spring the issues of life" (Proverbs 4:23, emp. added). Paul warned: "For those who live according to the flesh **set their minds** on the things of the flesh, but those who live according to the Spirit, the things of the Spirit. For to be **carnally minded** is death, but to be spiritually minded is life and peace" (Romans 8:5-6, emp. added). Listen carefully to Paul's description of the non-Christian mindset:

> This I say, therefore, and testify in the Lord, that you should no longer walk as the rest of the Gentiles walk, in the **futility of their mind**, having their understanding darkened, being alienated from the life of God, because of the ignorance that is in them, because of the hardening of their heart; who, being past feeling, have given themselves over to **lewdness**, to work all uncleanness with greediness. But you have not so learned Christ, if indeed you have heard Him and have been taught by Him, as the truth is in Jesus: that you put off, concerning your former conduct, the old man which grows corrupt according to the **deceitful lusts**, and be renewed in the spirit of your mind, and that you put on the new man which was created according to God, in true righteousness and holiness (Ephesians 4:17-24, emp. added).

Subjecting the mind to pornographic images facilitates its degeneration into futility.

The Proper View of Sex

Third, pornography is contrary to the Bible's elevated view of love, sex, and marriage. Instead, it cheapens and debases these noble, holy elements of human existence. It transforms sex into mindless, animalistic gratification and mere physical stimulation and pleasure. It thereby sidesteps the original purposes of sex established and intended by the Creator. Pornography dehumanizes women. It turns them into non-human objects. It eliminates the genuine, selfless love that should precede and presuppose sexual involvement (cf. Song of Solomon). Marriage is to be held in honor and conducted honorably (Hebrews 13:4; cf. Proverbs 5:15-23; 31:10-31).

To maintain a pure mind and life, we must "abhor what is evil" (Romans 12:9), that is, regard evil with horror and shrink with shuddering from it. We must "have no fellowship with the unfruitful works of darkness, but rather expose them. For it is shameful even to speak of those things which are done by them in secret" (Ephesians 5:11-12). To "expose" means to brand it as evil and show it for what it is. We must heed the advice of Paul to Timothy when he told him to keep himself pure (1 Timothy 5:22) and set an example in purity (1 Timothy 4:12). As John declared: "And everyone who has this hope in Him [of seeing Jesus–DM] purifies himself, just as He is pure" (1 John 3:3). To do otherwise is to "sow to the flesh." However, "he who sows to his flesh will of the flesh reap corruption, but he who sows to the Spirit will of the Spirit reap everlasting life" (Galatians 6:8). Peter urged the individual no longer to "live the rest of his time in the flesh for **the lusts of men**, but for the will of God. For we have spent enough of our past lifetime in doing the will of the Gentiles–when we walked in **lewdness, lusts…**" (1 Peter 4:2-3, emp. added). Paul concluded: "I say then: Walk in the Spirit, and you shall not fulfill **the lust of the flesh**" (Galatians 5:16, emp. added).

THE JUDICIAL SYSTEM

American civilization has strayed far away from its original moorings in the matter of pornography. It is amazing, appalling, and astonishing that in the last fifty years, the doors have been flung wide open to allow exhibition of pornography in many forms in many places–under the guise of "free speech" and constitutional rights. The courts that have countenanced and sanctioned such thinking have acted in diametric opposition to their judicial predecessors.

Consider, for example, the case of *The Commonwealth v. Sharpless*, in which the Supreme Court of Pennsylvania ruled in December of 1815. Here is the official description of the case:

> The Grand Inquest of the Commonwealth of Pennsylvania, inquiring for the city of Philadelphia, upon their oaths and affirmations respectively do present, that Jesse Sharpless, late of the same city yeoman, [et al.–DM], being evil disposed persons, and designing, contriving, and intending the morals, as well of youth as of divers other citizens of this commonwealth, to debauch and corrupt, and **to raise and create in their minds inordinate and lustful desires**, on the first day of March, in the year one thousand eight hundred and fifteen, at the city aforesaid, and within the jurisdiction of this Court, in a certain house, there situate, unlawfully, wickedly, and scandalously **did exhibit**, and show for money, to persons, to the inquest aforesaid unknown, **a certain lewd, wicked, scandalous, infamous, and obscene painting, representing a man in an obscene, impudent, and indecent posture with a woman**, to the manifest corruption and subversion of youth, and other citizens of this commonwealth, to the evil example of all others in like case offending, and against the peace and dignity of the commonwealth of Pennsylvania (*The Commonwealth...*, 1815, emp. added).

Interestingly, among the arguments offered by the Attorney General of Pennsylvania was the following: "It may be safely affirmed, that whatever tends to the destruction of morality in general, may be punished criminally. Crimes are public offences, not because they are perpetrated publicly, but because **their effect is to injure the public**" (*The Commonwealth...*, emp. added).

Having been convicted for displaying a pornographic painting in the privacy of their own home, the defendants were requesting that the State Supreme Court overturn their conviction. The majority opinion was written by Chief Justice Tilghman. The court was precise, pungent, and pointed: "Any offence which in its nature and by its example, tends to the corruption of morals, as the *exhibition of an obscene picture*, is indictable at common law" (*The Commonwealth...*, italics in orig.). Among other arguments, the court ruled that "[t]he courts are guardians of the public morals, and therefore have jurisdiction in such cases. Hence it follows, that an offence may be punishable, if in its nature and by its example, it tends to the corruption of morals, although it be not committed in public." Speaking directly to the issue of whether pornography is permissible if viewed in the privacy of one's own home, the court stated:

The mischief was no greater than if he had taken the purchaser into a *private room*, and sold him the book there. The law is not to be evaded by an artifice of that kind. **If the privacy of the room was a protection, all the youth of the city might be corrupted by taking them one by one into a chamber**, and there inflaming their passions by the exhibition of lascivious pictures (italics in orig., emp. added).

No man is permitted to corrupt the morals of the people. Secret poison cannot be thus disseminated. A slight knowledge of human nature teaches us, "that while secrecy is affected in a case like the present, public curiosity is more strongly excited thereby, and that those persons who may ignorantly suppose they have had the good fortune of seeing bawdy pictures, will not content themselves with keeping the secret in their own bosoms!" (emp. added).

The court also commented on the role of the courts in prosecuting cases of pornography:

The destruction of morality renders the power of the government invalid, for government is no more than public order. It weakens the bands by which society is kept together. The corruption of the public mind in general, and debauching the manners of youth in particular by lewd and obscene pictures exhibited to view, must necessarily be attended with the most injurious consequences, and in such instances **Courts of Justice are, or ought to be, the schools of morals** (emp. added).

The courts of America have certainly "dropped the ball" in abandoning their proper role and prostituting their original purpose. The sexual anarchy that runs rampant in the land is due partially to the failure of the courts to champion the cause of moral and sexual purity—as they were originally intended to do.

CONCLUSION

The glamorization of illicit sexual activity via pornography has fooled millions with its alluring mirage. But the **actual** results of the plague of pornography that has swept the land has been rampant venereal disease, broken marriages, shattered families, brokenness, addiction, depression, and suicide. The "free love" of the last 50 years has been neither free nor genuinely loving. The dehumanization of women in any culture contributes to men moving toward animalism and savagery, and eventually results in the breakdown of civilization. America is in serious trouble.

CHAPTER SIX

RESTORING SEXUAL SANITY: POSTPONING MORAL IMPLOSION

For over fifty years now, the Christian foundations of American civilization have been undergoing gradual, incessant erosion. The non-Christian forces of society, assisted in large measure by an unrestrained, leftist judiciary, have been systematically dismantling the nation's ties to the Bible, removing one by one the public symbols of America's Christian roots. The recent brouhaha over the phrase "under God" in the Pledge of Allegiance is simply one more example in a long series wherein the liberal forces, under the guise of "political correctness" and "separation of church and state" (a phrase not even found in the *Constitution*), are attempting to expunge all traces of America's Christian heritage. Make no mistake: the cultural fluctuation upon which the nation has embarked is a slippery slope that, if left unchecked, will guarantee America's downward spiral into the abyss of godless hedonism. The attack upon the external symbols that indicate attachment to God–from the Pledge or "In God We Trust" on coinage, to references to God in the *Declaration of Independence* or displays of the Ten Commandments in courthouses–is simply part of the larger conspiracy to act out hostility toward the God Who places restraints upon human behavior. American culture has literally been transformed into a **post**-Christian civilization.

SEXUAL ANARCHY

Many who have embraced the myth of a "religionless" society and government (interpreting "freedom of religion" to mean "freedom **from** religion" rather than "freedom **for** religion" as the Founding Fathers intended) have naively presumed that humans will automatically choose to do "right" (whatever "right" is), and that humans can be their own authority without any outside interference from a higher power imposing an objective standard upon them. They dispute the historical evidence that unrestrained freedom results in moral chaos and social anarchy.

Whereas Hinduism posits millions of gods (like all the pagan religions that have existed in human history–gods conjured up by their human creators and, hence, flawed like their creators), Buddhism removes humanity from the notion of higher powers "out there" to whom humans ought to look for guidance, and places divinity within each individual. Hence, every human has within himself/herself sufficient insight into "right" if he or she can just "get in touch" with the "inner self." [NOTE: The Bible alludes to such thinking in the phrase, "everyone did what was right in his own eyes" (Judges 21:25).] To fail to connect with the inner self is to be subjected to a virtually endless cycle of reliving earthly existence through an infinite number of life forms (animal and plant) until one learns his or her lesson and "gets it right."

American civilization has been the victim of serious encroachment by this secular "New Age" philosophy. In sharp contradistinction, the Founding Fathers of America were adamant in their insistence that **Christianity must remain the moral and spiritual foundation of America**. Let us remind ourselves again what George Washington said, after serving two terms as President of the United States, in his farewell address to the Nation:

> Of all the dispositions and habits which lead to political prosperity, **religion and morality** are indispensable supports. In vain would that man claim the tribute of patriotism, who should labor to subvert **these great pillars of human happiness**, these firmest props of the duties of men and citizens.... **Reason and experience both forbid us to expect that national morality can prevail in exclusion of religious principle** (1796a, emp. added).

RESTORING SEXUAL SANITY:
POSTPONING MORAL IMPLOSION

The second president of these United States held the same viewpoint. After serving two terms as vice president alongside President George Washington, on October 11, 1798, John Adams affirmed: "[W]e have no government armed with power capable of contending with human passions unbridled by morality and religion.... **Our Constitution was made only for a moral and religious people.** It is wholly inadequate to the government of any other" (1854, 9:229, emp. added).

Observe that the Framers and Founders went on record, stating that should this country ever abandon the Christian religion and Christian morality, the nation would be subject to inevitable collapse. Signer of the federal *Constitution* and Secretary of War under both Presidents Washington and Adams, James McHenry insisted:

> The Holy Scriptures....can alone secure to society, order and peace, and to our courts of justice and constitutions of government, purity, stability, and usefulness. In vain, without the Bible, we increase penal laws and draw entrenchments around our institutions. Bibles are strong entrenchments. Where they abound, men cannot pursue wicked courses (as quoted in Steiner, 1921, p. 14).

Joseph Story, a Father of American Jurisprudence and U.S. Supreme Court justice for 34 years (having been appointed by President James Madison), claimed that "it is impossible for those who believe in the truth of Christianity as a Divine revelation, to doubt that it is the especial duty of government to foster and encourage it among all the citizens and subjects" (1833, 3:723).

Even the courts of America once declared in no uncertain terms the essentiality of Christian morality to the fabric of American civilization; "No free government now exists in the world unless where Christianity is acknowledged and is the religion of the country" (*Updegraph v. The Commonwealth*, 1824). In 1811, the New York State Supreme Court declared that "whatever strikes at the root of Christianity tends manifestly to the dissolution of civil government.... [W]e are a Christian people, and the morality of the country is deeply engrafted upon Christianity (*People v. Ruggles*, 1811). And in 1846, the direction of our nation was unwittingly forecast in the following words: "What constitutes the standard of good morals? Is it not Christianity? There certainly is none other.... The day of moral virtue in which we live would, in an instant, if that standard were abolished, lapse into the dark and murky night of pagan immorality" (*City Council of Charleston v. Benjamin*). With almost haunting, prophetic anticipation, Daniel Webster predicted in 1852 what would happen if America ever strayed away from the religious heritage on which she was founded:

> If we and our posterity reject religious instruction and authority, violate the rules of eternal justice, trifle with the injunctions of morality, and recklessly destroy the political constitution which holds us together, no man can tell how sudden a catastrophe may overwhelm us that shall bury all our glory in profound obscurity (1903, 13:492-493).

One could not find a more accurate description of precisely what has been happening in America for the last fifty years.

Calvin Coolidge, the 30th president of the United States, expressed the sentiments of the Founders when he stated: "The foundation of our society and our government rests so much on **the teaching of the Bible** that it would be difficult to support these foundations if faith in these teachings would cease to be practically universal in our country" ("Coolidge-Bible," 2004, emp. added). As French historian Alexis de Tocqueville observed in his remarks regarding America in the 1830s: "How is it possible that society should **escape destruction** if the moral tie is not strengthened in proportion as the political tie is relaxed? And what can be done with a people who are their own masters if they are not submissive to the Deity?" (1945, p. 307). The moral tie of America has been significantly weakened over the past 50 years. If Tocqueville, and these American predecessors were correct, America is moving swiftly toward destruction.

The only rational perspective is the biblical one, the one upon which this nation was founded—that one Supreme Being exists Who is nonphysical (i.e., spirit—John 4:24), transcendent of the physical realm, and infinite in all of His attributes. No other rational explanation exists for what we observe all around us. Evolution certainly does not account for it. No atheist, mystic, evolutionist, or existential philosopher has come up with an adequate explanation. The evidence points to the existence of God—the God described on the pages of the Bible. As the Creator, He has communicated to humans regarding their origin, their purpose in life, and their eternal destiny. Those who wish to be free from restraint in order to indulge their sexual appetites may invent complex, convoluted alternate explanations for human existence, and they may insist that moral behavior is subjective and susceptible to the whim of human inclination, but no such evasions will alter the facts. Those who remain rational, objective, and unbiased are forced to conclude that spiritual reality is within the grasp of every accountable human being. But the individual must decide to seek the truth.

So the fact remains that there is a God in heaven (Daniel 2:28). God has spoken to the human race through His written Word, i.e., the Bible. In that inspired communication, He has designated the structure of society. He created male and female with the intention for one man to marry one woman for life (Genesis 2:24; Matthew 19:4-6). Here is the foundational building block of humanity. That is His simple will on the matter. He hates divorce (Malachi 2:16). The only way He permits divorce is if one marriage partner divorces the other marriage partner for the one reason that the marriage partner has committed fornication, i.e., illicit sexual intercourse. Upon that basis alone, God allows the innocent partner to put away that unfaithful mate and form a second marriage with an eligible partner (Matthew 19:3-9).

God intended for the husband and wife to produce children who, in turn, are to receive nurturing and care from their parents in a stable, loving home (Ephesians 6:1-4; Colossians 3:18-21). In this divinely ordained institution of the home, God intended that children receive the necessary instruction and training to prepare them to be productive, honest, God-fearing, hard-working citizens of their country. The home was designed by God to impart to each succeeding generation proper religious, moral, and social principles that would in turn make the nation strong and virtuous. The Bible is filled with references to the essential ingredients of healthy family life (e.g., Deuteronomy 4:7-9; 6:1-9; 11:18-21; 32:46-47; Psalm 127; Proverbs 5:15-20; 6:20-35; 11: 29; 12:4; 14:1; 15:25,27; 17:1,13; 31:10-31), including proper parenting skills (Proverbs 13:24; 19:18; 22:15; 23:13-14; 29:15, 17; Ephesians 6:1-4). Parents simply must bring their own lives into harmony with God's Word—and then be about the business of training their children to do likewise. The bulk of society's ills would be rectified if this simple formula for national health were reinstated in America.

Our sex-crazed society is so promiscuous, and so estranged from God's view of human sexuality, that our public schools consider it appropriate to teach children to simply "take precautions" when they engage in sexual escapades outside of marriage. But God **never** encouraged people to practice that kind of "safe sex." The Bible definition of "safe sex" is sex that is confined to a divinely authorized, scriptural marriage (1 Corinthians 7:2-5). God insists that people can, and must, exercise self-control, self-discipline, and moral responsibility. The Bible teaches that we are not to be self-indulgent. We are to put restraints on ourselves, controlling our sexual urges in accordance with God's teachings.

Encouraging young people simply to "take precautions" only encourages additional illicit behavior. It encourages more promiscuity. It contributes to an increase—not a decrease—in the number of pregnancies and sexually transmitted diseases. Despite several decades of inundating our schools with sex education and the promotion of so-called "safe sex," statisticians inform us that in 2004, childbearing by unmarried women reached a record high of almost 1.5 million births, with more than 4 in 5 births to teenagers being nonmarital, and 35.7 % of all births being to unmarried women (Hamilton, et al.). The social liberals' "solution" has not worked. In fact, the problem has been greatly exacerbated.

The depths to which our country has slumped morally is evinced by the legality of the distribution of birth-control devices to students, and the **illegality** of the distribution of Bibles (or teaching Bible principles). The time has come for our nation to wake up, and for all citizens to understand that **freedom requires restraint.** Rights require personal responsibility. People must take responsibility for their personal choices, and must accept the consequences of their own actions. Paul declared: "flee fornication" (1 Corinthians 6:18). He did not write, "engage in 'safe' fornication"! There is no such thing as "safe" sin or "safe" immorality, because all sin is damning (James 1:15). God said a person must run away from it, resist it, and reject it (2 Corinthians 6:18). To a young man, Paul said: "Keep yourself pure" (1 Timothy 5:22). The writer of Hebrews insisted that the marriage bed is to be kept "undefiled." "[F]ornicators and adulterers God will judge" (Hebrews 13:4). There should not be so much as a hint of sexual immorality among Christians (Ephesians 5:3).

It is absolutely necessary to come to grips with certain eternal realities. Since sufficient evidence exists by which one can know that God exists (see Warren, 1972; Flew and Warren, 1977; Thompson, 2000), and since one can know that God has spoken to human beings by means of the inspired, infallible, inerrant, authoritative Word of God, i.e., the Bible, then it necessarily follows that moral choices and human behavior are to be governed by that revealed will. Pre-marital, extra-marital, and homosexual sex are out of harmony with God's will.

One would do well to give serious contemplation to the straightforward pronouncements regarding sexual behavior from the wisest man to live on Earth:

> My son, pay attention to my wisdom; lend your ear to my understanding,
>
> That you may preserve discretion, and your lips may keep knowledge.

For the lips of an immoral woman drip honey, and her mouth is smoother than oil;

But in the end she is bitter as wormwood, sharp as a two-edged sword.

Her feet go down to death, her steps lay hold of hell.

Lest you ponder her path of life–her ways are unstable; you do not know them (Proverbs 5:1-6)

Drink water from your own cistern, and running water from your own well.

Should your fountains be dispersed abroad, streams of water in the streets?

Let them be only your own, and not for strangers with you.

Let your fountain be blessed, and rejoice with the wife of your youth.

As a loving deer and a graceful doe, let her breasts satisfy you at all times;

and always be enraptured with her love.

For why should you, my son, be enraptured by an immoral woman,

and be embraced in the arms of a seductress?

For the ways of man are before the eyes of the Lord, and He ponders all his paths.

His own iniquities entrap the wicked man, and he is caught in the cords of his sin.

He shall die for lack of instruction, and in the greatness of his folly he shall go astray (Proverbs 5:15-23).

For the commandment is a lamp, and the law a light; reproofs of instruction are the way of life,

To keep you from the evil woman, from the flattering tongue of a seductress.

Do not lust after her beauty in your heart, nor let her allure you with her eyelids.

For by means of a harlot a man is reduced to a crust of bread;

And an adulteress will prey upon his precious life.

Can a man take fire to his bosom, and his clothes not be
burned?

Can one walk on hot coals, and his feet not be seared?

So is he who goes in to his neighbor's wife; whoever touches
her shall not be innocent.

People do not despise a thief if he steals to satisfy himself
when he is starving.

Yet when he is found, he must restore sevenfold; he may
have to give up all the substance of his house.

Whoever commits adultery with a woman lacks understanding; he who does so destroys his own soul.

Wounds and dishonor he will get, and his reproach will
not be wiped away.

For jealousy is a husband's fury; therefore he will not
spare in the day of vengeance.

He will accept no recompense, nor will he be appeased
though you give many gifts (Proverbs 6:23-35).

These admonitions are crisp and timely for our own culture. Much
more wisdom is found in the Bible concerning the temptations
of illicit sexual activity (e.g., Proverbs 7). But notice that we have
been warned. God has forewarned and forearmed us for facing
life. But we must have the gumption, the integrity, and the character to heed His admonitions. He will not coerce anyone to do
His will. Conforming to the Creator's will regarding human sexuality is not "moral repression" or "erotophobic provincialism."
Conformity may well stifle "political correctness." But His in-
structions will give life and bring happiness (Psalm 119).

And there is no time to lose. God will tolerate depravity only
so long. As George Washington warned in his first inaugural address delivered in New York City on Thursday, April 30, 1789:
"[W]e ought to be no less persuaded that the propitious smiles of
Heaven can never be expected on a nation that disregards the
eternal rules of order and right which Heaven itself has ordained"
(1796b). Or, to put it more bluntly, consider Thomas Jefferson's
warning regarding immorality: "I tremble for my country when

I reflect that God is just: that **His justice cannot sleep forever**" (1794, XVIII, p. 237, emp. added).

John Adams, the first vice president of the United States, and one who had much to do with the writing of the constitution of the Commonwealth of Massachusetts, offered these virtually prophetic words in 1763 that ought to haunt, if not shame, those who are participants in the sexual anarchy that has gripped America:

> [D]emocracy will soon degenerate into an anarchy, **such an anarchy that every man will do what is right in his own eyes** and no man's life or property or reputation or liberty will be secure, and every one of these will soon mould itself into **a system of subordination of all the moral virtues** and intellectual abilities, all the powers of wealth, beauty, wit, and science, **to the wanton pleasures**, the capricious will, and the execrable cruelty of one or **a very few** (1807, 1:83, emp. added).

Benjamin Franklin echoed these very sentiments in a letter to Thomas Paine in which he took issue with Paine's thoughts on whether a "particular Providence," i.e., the God of the Bible, existed:

> [Y]ou strike at the foundations of all religion. For without the belief of a Providence that takes cognizance of, guards, and guides, and may favor particular persons, there is no motive to worship a Deity, to fear his displeasure, or to pray for his protection…. [T]hink how great a portion of mankind…have need of the motives of religion to restrain them from vice, to support their virtue, and retain them in the practice of it till it becomes habitual, which is the great point for its security…. **If men are so wicked *with* religion, what would they be if without it?** (1840, 10:281-282, emp. and italics added).

What would our Founding Fathers say if they knew that American society would one day tolerate (and even countenance) not only homosexuality between consenting adults, but also pedophilia, incest, and bestiality? In the introduction to his book, *Understanding Loved Boys and Boylovers*, David Riegel claims that men who become involved in sexual relationships with boys "are sincere, concerned, loving human beings who simply have–and were probably born with–a sexual orientation that is neither understood nor accepted by most others" (as quoted in Moore, 2002). What would the Founders say about the availability of pedophilic books like *Varieties of Man/Boy Love* and *Enchanted Love*, and organizations like NAMBLA (North American Man/Boy Love Association)? Or books that extol incest like *Daddy, An Erotic Memoir* (Martin, 2000)? And what would they say if they knew that we now countenance sexual relations with animals–as advocated in books like *Dearest Pet: On Bestiality* and *The Horseman: Obsessions of a Zoophile*? They would be dumbfounded, incredulous–and horrified at the unbridled, rampant sexual anarchy.

Divorce, abortion, homosexuality, pornography, pedophilia, incest, bestiality. The solution to the moral confusion and sexual corruption that has gripped American civilization is simple–if hearts are humbly yielded to the will of God. If we could get our families back on track according to God's will, we could get our nation back on track. It starts with you and me. We must embrace Bible teaching regarding human sexuality. Then we must be about the business of encouraging others to do the same–before wickedness destroys our nation.

If My people who are called by My name will humble themselves, and pray and seek My face, and turn from their wicked ways, then I will hear from heaven, and will forgive their sin and heal their land.... But if you turn away and forsake My statutes and My commandments which I have set before you...then I will uproot them from My land which I have given them; and this house which I have sanctified for My name I will cast out of My sight, and will make it a proverb and a byword among all peoples (2 Chronicles 7:14,19-20).

The Lord brings the counsel of the nations to nothing; He makes the plans of the peoples of no effect. The counsel of the Lord stands forever, the plans of His heart to all generations. Blessed is the nation whose God is the Lord (Psalm 33:10-12).

Righteousness exalts a nation, but sin is a reproach to any people (Proverbs 14:34).

REFERENCES

"Abortion" (2004), *The Polling Report*, [On-line], : http://www.pol lingreport.com/abortion.htm.

"Abortion in the United States: Statistics and Trends," (2005), *National Right to Life*, [On-line], URL: http://www.nrlc.org/ abortion/facts/abortionstats.html.

Adams, John (1807), *The Papers of John Adams*, ed. Robert Taylor (Cambridge: Belknap Press, 1977 reprint).

Adams, John (1854), *The Works of John Adams, Second President of the United States*, ed. Charles Adams (Boston, MA: Little, Brown, and Company).

Adams, John and Samuel Adams (1802), *Four Letters: Being an Interesting Correspondence Between Those Eminently Distinguished Characters, John Adams, Late President of the United States; and Samuel Adams, Late Governor of Massachusetts. On the Important Subject of Government* (Boston, MA: Adams and Rhoades).

Adams, John Quincy (1821), *Address Delivered at the Request of the Committee of Arrangements for Celebrating the Anniversary of Independence at the City of Washington on the Fourth of July 1821, Upon the Occasion of Reading the Declaration of Independence* (Cambridge, MA: Hilliard and Metcalf).

Alan Guttmacher Institute (2002), "Induced Abortion," [On-line], URL: http://www.agi-usa.org/pubs/fb_induced_abortion.pdf.

Alford, Henry (1875), *Greek Testament* (Grand Rapids, MI: Baker, 1980 reprint).

American Heritage Dictionary of the English Language (2000), (Boston, MA: Houghton Mifflin), fourth edition.

American Psychiatric Association Public Information (2002), "Gay and Lesbian Issues," [On-line], URL: http://www.psych.org/public_info/homose-1.cfm.

Archer, Gleason L. Jr. (1982), *An Encyclopedia of Bible Difficulties* (Grand Rapids, MI: Zondervan).

Arndt, William and F.W. Gingrich (1957), *A Greek-English Lexicon of the New Testament and Other Early Christian Literature* (Chicago, IL: University of Chicago Press).

"Bald Eagle" (2002), [On-line], URL: http://midwest.fws.gov/eagle/protect/laws.html.

Barclay, William (1958), *The Letters of John and Jude* (Philadelphia, PA: Westminster).

Barnes, Albert (1978 reprint), *Notes on the New Testament: James, Peter, John, and Jude* (Grand Rapids, MI: Baker).

Barton, David (2000), *Original Intent* (Aledo, TX: Wallbuilder Press), third edition.

Bengel, John Albert (1971), *New Testament Word Studies*, trans. Charlton Lewis and Marvin Vincent (Grand Rapids, MI: Kregel).

Bergman, J. (1986), *"yada,"* *Theological Dictionary of the Old Testament*, ed. G. Johannes Botterweck and Helmer Ringgren (Grand Rapids, MI: Eerdmans).

Beyer, Hermann (1964), *"heteros,"* *Theological Dictionary of the New Testament*, ed. Gerhard Kittel (Grand Rapids, MI:Eerdmans, 1982 reprint).

"'Bible as Hate Speech' Signed into Law" (2004), *World Net Daily*, April 20, [On-line], URL: http://www.worldnetdaily.com/news/article.asp?ARTICLE_ID=38268.

"Bible Verses Regarded as Hate Literature" (2003), *World Net Daily*, February 18, [On-line], URL: http://www.worldnet daily.com/news/article.asp?ARTICLE_ID=31080.

REFERENCES

Blackstone, William (1765-1769), *Commentaries on the Laws of England* (Oxford: Clarendon Press), [On-line], URL: http://www. lonang.com/exlibris/blackstone/.

Bloom, Allan (1987), *The Closing of the American Mind* (New York: Simon and Schuster).

Bork, Robert (1996), *Slouching Towards Gomorrah* (New York: Regan-Books).

"Born Again Christians Just As Likely To Divorce As Non-Christians" (2004), *The Barna Update*, [On-line], URL: http://www. barna.org/FlexPage.aspx?page=BarnaUpdate&BarnaUp dateID=170.

Botterweck, G. Johannes (1986), "*yada*," *Theological Dictionary of the Old Testament*, ed. G. Johannes Botterweck and Helmer Ringgren (Grand Rapids, MI: Eerdmans).

Bowers v. Hardwick, et al. (1986), [On-line], URL: http://caselaw. lp.findlaw.com/scripts/getcase.pl?navby=case&court=us& vol=478&page=186.

Brown, Abram English (1898), *John Hancock, His Book* (Boston, MA: Lee and Shepard).

Brown, Francis, S.R. Driver, and Charles A. Briggs (1906), *The Brown-Driver-Briggs Hebrew and English Lexicon* (Peabody, MA: Hendrickson, 2000 reprint).

Cameron, Paul, William L. Playfair, and Stephen Wellum (1993), "The Homosexual Lifespan," paper presented at Eastern Psychological Association, April 17.

Carr, David (2003), "Chapter and Verse," [On-line], URL: http: //www.pbs.org/pov/pov2003/familyfundamentals/special_ chapter_3.html.

"Causes of Pelvic Inflammatory Disease" (2003), [On-line], URL: http://www.wrongdiagnosis.com/p/pelvic_inflammatory_ disease/causes.htm.

"Child Fatalities Fact Sheet" (2003), *National Clearinghouse on Child Abuse and Neglect Information*, [On-line], URL: http:// nccanch.acf.hhs.gov/pubs/factsheets/fatality.cfm.

City Council of Charleston v. S.A. Benjamin (1846), 2 Strob. 508 (Sup. Ct. SC 1846).

Clarke, Adam (no date), *Clarke's Commentary: Genesis-Deuteronomy* (New York: Abingdon-Cokesbury).

The Commonwealth v. Sharpless (1815), Supreme Court of Pennsylvania, Eastern District, Philadelphia, 2 Serg. & Rawle 91; 1815 Pa. LEXIS 81.

"Coolidge-Bible" (2004), Minnesota Family Council, [On-line], URL: http://www.mfc.org/contents/transcript.asp?id=996.

Cranfield, C.E.B. (1985), *A Critical and Exegetical Commentary on the Epistle to the Romans*, ed. J.A. Emmerton and C.E.B. Cranfield (Edinburgh: Clark).

Davis v. Beason (1889), Supreme Court of the United States, 133 U.S. 333; 10 5. Ct. 299; 33 L. Ed. 637; 1890 U.S. LEXIS 1915.

Deyoung, James B. (1988), "The Meaning of 'Nature' in Romans and Its Implications for Biblical Proscriptions of Homosexual Behavior," *Journal of the Evangelical Theological Society* 31: 429-441.

Duin, Julia (2003), "Gay Bishop Sets Off Talk of Episcopal Schism," *The Washington Times*, [On-line], URL: http://www.dyn amic. washtimes.com/print_story.cfm?StoryID=20030806-123 147-7931r.

Fagan, Amy (2003), "Ban Nears on Partial-birth Abortion," *The Washington Times*, [On-line], URL: http://washingtontimes. com/national/20030917-104555-1303r.htm.

Falkenroth, Ulrich (1978), "Punishment," *The New International Dictionary of New Testament Theology*, ed. Colin Brown (Grand Rapids, MI: Zondervan).

Finer, Lawrence B. and Stanley K. Henshaw (2003), "Abortion Incidence and Services in the United States in 2000," [On-line], URL: http://www.agi-usa.org/pubs/journals/3500 603.pdf.

Fishbane, Michael (1985), *Biblical Interpretation in Ancient Israel* (New York: Oxford University Press).

Flatt, Bill, Jack Lewis, and Dowell Flatt (1982), *Counseling Homosexuals* (Jonesboro, AR: National Christian Press).

Flew, Antony G.N. and Thomas B. Warren (1977), *Warren-Flew Debate* (Jonesboro, AR: National Christian Press).

Franklin, Benjamin (1749), *Proposals Relating to the Education of Youth in Pennsylvania* (Philadelphia, PA).

Franklin, Benjamin (1840), *The Works of Benjamin Franklin*, ed. Jared Sparks (Boston, MA: Tappan, Whittemore, and Mason).

Gersten, Dennis (no date), "The Modern Oath of Hippocrates," [On-line], URL: http://www.imagerynet.com/hippo.ama.html.

Gesenius, William (1847), *Hebrew-Chaldee Lexicon to the Old Testament* (Grand Rapids, MI: Baker), 1979 reprint.

Gibbon, Edward (1776), *The History of the Decline and Fall of the Roman Empire*, "Progress of the Christian Religion," [On-line], URL: http://www.bibliomania.com/2/1/62/109/frameset.html.

Greenhouse, Linda (2004), "Court Overrules Law Restricting Cable Sex Shows," *The New York Times On the Web*, [On-line], URL: http://www.nytimes.com/library/politics/scotus/articles/052300scotus.html.

Hagelin, Rebecca (2004), "Overdosing on Porn," [On-line], URL: http://www.worldandi.com.

Hamilton, Brady, et al. (2004), "Preliminary Births for 2004," *National Center for Health Statistics*, [On-line], URL: http://www.cdc.gov/nchs/products/pubs/pubd/hestats/prelim_births/prelim_births04.htm.

Harris, R. Laird (1990), *The Expositor's Bible Commentary: Leviticus*, ed. Frank Gaebelein (Grand Rapids, MI: Zondervan).

Harris, R. Laird, Gleason Archer, Jr. and Bruce Waltke, eds. (1980), *Theological Wordbook of the Old Testament* (Chicago, IL: Moody).

Harrub, Brad, Bert Thompson, and Dave Miller (2004), "'This is the Way God Made Me'—A Scientific Examination of Homosexuality and the 'Gay Gene,'" *Reason & Revelation*, 24:73-79, August.

Hasel, G.F. (1995), "*karat,*" *Theological Dictionary of the Old Testament*, ed. G. Johannes Botterweck, Helmer Ringgren, and Heinz-Josef Fabry (Grand Rapids, MI: Eerdmans).

Hauck, F. (1967), "*miaino,*" *Theological Dictionary of the New Testament*, ed. Gerhard Kittel (Grand Rapids, MI:Eerdmans, 1981 reprint).

Herek, Gregory (2002), "Facts About Homosexuality and Mental Health," [On-line], URL:http://psychology.ucdavis.edu/rainbow/html/facts_mental_health.html.

"The Hippocratic Oath" (1998), [On-line], URL: http://members.tripod.com/nktiuro/hippocra.htm.

"Human Genome Report Press Release" (2003), International Consortium Completes Human Genome Project, [On-line], URL: http://www.ornl.gov/TechResources/Human_Genome/project/50yr.html.

"Is Homosexual Marriage a Constitutional Right?" (2003), *The Bill of Rights Institute*, [On-line], URL: http://www.billofrightsinstitute.org/print.php?sid=430.

Jamieson, Robert, A.R. Fausset, and David Brown (no date), *A Commentary on the Old and New Testaments* (Grand Rapids, MI: Zondervan).

Jefferson, Thomas (1794), *Notes on the State of Virginia* (Philadelphia, PA: Mathew Carey).

Jefferson, Thomas (1903-1904), *Writings of Thomas Jefferson*, ed. Albert Bergh (Washington, DC: Thomas Jefferson Memorial Association).

"Judge Blocks Partial-Birth Abortion Ban" (2004), *Fox News*, [On-line]: URL: http://www.foxnews.com/story/0,2933,121435,00.html.

Kaiser, Walter (1990), *The Expositor's Bible Commentary: Exodus*, ed. Frank Gaebelein (Grand Rapids, MI: Zondervan).

REFERENCES

Kass, Leon (2002), *Human Cloning and Human Dignity* (New York: PublicAffairs).

Keil, C.F. and F. Delitzsch (1976 reprint), *Commentary on the Old Testament: The Pentateuch* (Grand Rapids, MI: Eerdmans).

Kiely, Kathy (2003), "Senate Okays Partial Birth Abortion Ban," [On-line], URL: http://www.usatoday.com/news/Washington/2003-03-13-abortion-bill x.htm.

Knight, G.A.F. (1981), *Leviticus* (Louisville, KY: Westminster John Knox Press).

LaRue, Jan (2003), "Trash Babies: A Legacy of 30 Years of Roe v. Wade," [On-line], URL: http://www.cwfa.org/articledisplay. asp?id=3151&department=CWA&categoryid=life.

Lawrence, et al. v. Texas (2003), [On-line], URL: http://caselaw. lp.findlaw.com/cgi-bin/getcase.pl?court=US&navby=case& vol=000&invol=02-102.

Lenski, R.C.H. (1951), *The Interpretation of St. Paul's Epistle to the Romans* (Columbus, OH: Wartburg).

Lenski, R.C.H. (1966), *The Interpretation of the Epistles of St. Peter, St. John, and St. Jude* (Minneapolis, MN: Augsburg).

Limbacher, Carl (2003), "Monument to Homosexuals Is OK; Monument to Ten Commandments Isn't," [On-line], URL: http://www.newsmax.com/archives/ic/2003/8/27/142215. shtml.

Lyons, Eric and Bert Thompson (2002), "In the 'Image and Likeness of God,' " *Reason & Revelation*, March, 22[3]:17-23 and April, 22[4]:25-31, [On-line]: URL: http://www.apologetics press.org/rr/rr2002/r&r0203a.htm.

Macknight, James (no date), *Apostolical Epistles* (Grand Rapids, MI: Baker).

Martin, Judith (2000), "Christian Activists Boycott Amazon.com," [On-line], URL: http://www.bookflash.com/releases/100 240.html.

Mayor, J.B. (no date), *The Expositor's Greek Testament: Jude*, ed. W. Robertson Nicoll (Grand Rapids, MI: Eerdmans).

McCord, Hugo (no date), "When Does Life Begin?" in *Fifty Years of Lectures* (Atwood, TN: Church of Christ).

"Mini-Britneys" (2004), *The Washington Times*, 3-9, May.

Moore, Art (2002), "Amazon.com Accused of Aiding Molesters," *WorldNetDaily*, [On-line], URL: http://www.worldnetdaily.com/news/article.asp?ARTICLE_ID=29065%20.

"More TV Sex" (2000), *USA Today*, March 30.

Moulton, James and George Milligan (1930), *Vocabulary of the Greek New Testament Illustrated from the Papyri and Other Non-literary Sources* (Grand Rapids, MI: Eerdmans, 1982 reprint).

Moulton, W.F., A.S. Geden, and H.K. Moulton (1978), *A Concordance to the Greek Testament* (Edinburgh: T.&T. Clark), fifth edition.

"New look at TV Sex and Violence" (2000), *National Catholic Register*, 16-22, April.

"Pelvic Inflammatory Disease" (1998), National Institutes of Health, [On-line], URL: http://www.niaid.nih.gov/factsheets/stdpid.htm.

"Pelvic Inflammatory Disease" (2001), *Joseph F. Smith Medical Library*, [On-line], URL: http://www.chclibrary.org/micromed/00060140.html.

The People v. Ruggles (1811), Supreme Court of New York, 8 Johns. 290; 1811 N.Y. LEXIS 124.

Perschbacher, Wesley ed. (1990), *The New Analytical Greek Lexicon* (Peabody, MA: Hendrickson).

Pfeiffer, Charles (1957), *The Book of Leviticus* (Grand Rapids, MI: Baker).

"PID" (2004), *Health Communities*, [On-line], URL: http://www.womenshealthchannel.com/pid/index.shtml.

Popenoe, David and Barbara Dafoe Whitehead (1999), "What's Happening to Marriage?" [On-line], URL: http//marriage. Rutgers.edu/Publications/pubwhatshappening.htm.

"Pornography Statistics 2003" (2004), *Family Safe Media*, [On-line], URL: http://www.familysafemedia.com/pornography_statistics.html.

Reagan, Ronald (1984), *Abortion and the Conscience of the Nation* (Nashville, TN: Thomas Nelson).

"Reasons For Movie Ratings" (2000), *The Classification and Rating Administration*, [On-line], URL: http://www.filmratings.com.

"Resident Population by States: 2000" (2000), [On-line], URL: http://www.hawaii.gov/dbedt/census2k/c2-4-rank.html.

Robertson, A.T. (1934), *A Grammar of the Greek New Testament in the Light of Historical Research* (Nashville, TN: Broadman Press).

Robinson, B.A. (2003), "Criminalizing Same-Sex Behavior," [On-line], URL: http://www.religioustolerance.org/hom_laws1.htm.

Roe v. Wade, 410 U.S. 113 (1973), [On-line], URL: http://caselaw.lp.findlaw.com/scripts/getcase.pl?court=US&vol=410&invol=113.

Rush, Benjamin (1798), "Defense of the Use of the Bible as a School Book," *Essays, Literary, Moral and Philosophical* (Philadelphia, PA: Thomas & Samuel F. Bradford).

Salmond, S.D.F. (1950), *The Pulpit Commentary–Jude*, ed. H.D.M. Spence and Joseph S. Exell (Grand Rapids, MI: Eerdmans).

Schneider, Johannes (1964), "*erchomai,*" *Theological Dictionary of the New Testament*, ed. Gerhard Kittel (Grand Rapids, MI: Eerdmans, 1982 reprint).

Schreiner, J. (1990), "*yalad,*" *Theological Dictionary of the Old Testament*, ed. G. Johannes Botterweck and Helmer Ringgren (Grand Rapids, MI: Eerdmans).

Seesemann, Heinrich (1967), *"opiso," Theological Dictionary of the New Testament,* ed. Gerhard Friedrich (Grand Rapids, MI: Eerdmans, 1981 reprint).

"Sex on TV: Content and Context" (2001), *The Kaiser Family Foundation,* February 5.

"Sexuality, Contraception, and the Media" (2001), *American Academy of Pediatrics Committee on Public Education,* January.

Snyder, K. Alan (1990), *Defining Noah Webster: Mind and Morals in the Early Republic* (New York, NY: University Press of America).

"Sodomy Laws in the United States" (2003), [On-line], URL: http://www.sodomylaws.org/usa/usa.htm.

Sparks, Jared (1860), *Lives of William Pinkney, William Ellery, and Cotton Mather* (New York: Harper and Brothers).

Steiner, Bernard C. (1907), *The Life and Correspondence of James McHenry* (Cleveland, OH: Burrows Brothers).

Steiner, Bernard C. (1921), *One Hundred and Ten years of Bible Society Work in Maryland, 1810-1920* (Baltimore, MD: The Maryland Bible Society).

Story, Joseph (1833), *Commentaries on the Constitution of the United States* (Boston, MA: Hillard, Gray, & Co.).

"Study Links TV to Teen Sexual Activity" (2004), [On-line], URL: www.cnn.com/2004/HEALTH/09/07/tv.teen. sex.reut/index.html.

Tertullian (1973 reprint), *The Ante-Nicene Fathers,* ed. Alexander Roberts and James Donaldson (Grand Rapids, MI: Eerdmans).

"Texas Mother Charged With Killing Her 5 Children," (2001), *Cable News Network,* [On-line], URL: http://www.cnn.com/2001/US/06/20/children.killed/, June 21.

Thayer, Joseph H. (1901), *A Greek-English Lexicon of the New Testament* (Grand Rapids, MI: Baker, 1977 reprint).

Thompson, Bert (2000), *Rock-Solid Faith: How to Build It* (Montgomery, AL: Apologetics press).

Thompson, Bert (2004), *The Christian and Medical Ethics* (Montgomery, AL: Apologetics Press), third edition.

Tippens, Darryl (2000), "Not Voice of ACU," *Abilene Reporter-News*, November 21.

Tocqueville, Alexis de (1945 reprint), *Democracy in America* (New York, NY: Alfred A. Knopf).

"Transcript: Justice Moore on His Monumental Battle," *Fox News*, [On-line], URL: http://www.foxnews.com/story/0,2933,95342, 00.html.

"TV Sex Getting 'Safer'" (2003), *Kaiser Family Foundation*, [On-line], URL: www.kff.org.

"The U.S. Constitution Online" (no date), [On-line], URL: http: //www.usconstitution.net/const.html#Am5.

United States: Uniform Crime Report–State Statistics from 1960-2000 (2000), The Disaster Center, [On-line], URL: http://www.di sastercenter.com/crime/.

Updegraph v. The Commonwealth (1824), Supreme Court of Pennsylvania, Western District, Pittsburgh, 11 Serg. & Rawle 394; 1824 Pa. LEXIS 85.

VanGemeren, Willem, ed. (1997), *New International Dictionary of Old Testament Theology and Exegesis* (Grand Rapids, MI: Zondervan).

Warren, Thomas B. (1972), *Have Atheists Proved There Is No God?* (Jonesboro, AR: National Christian Press).

Washington, George (1796a), "Farewell Address," *The Avalon Project at Yale University*, [On-line], URL: http://www.yale.edu/ lawweb/avalon/washing.htm.

Washington, George (1796b), "First Inaugural Address of George Washington," *The Avalon Project at Yale University*, [On-line], URL: http://www.yale.edu/lawweb/avalon/presiden/inaug/wash1 .htm.

Washington, George (1932), *The Writings of Washington*, ed. John C. Fitzpatrick (Washington, D.C.: U.S. Government Printing Office).

Webster, Daniel (1903), *The Writings and Speeches of Daniel Webster* (Boston, MA: Little, Brown, & Co.).

Webster, Noah (1857), *The Elementary Spelling Book* (New York: American Book Company).

Wenham, Gordon (1979), *The Book of Leviticus* (Grand Rapids, MI: Eerdmans).

West, D. Gene (2004), "Homosexuality, Alternative or Deviate Lifestyle" [a tract], (Moundsville, WV).

Whitehead, Barbara (1993), "Dan Quayle Was Right," *The Atlantic Monthly*, [On-line], URL: http://www.theatlantic.com/politics/family/danquayl.htm.

Whitelaw, Thomas (1950), *The Pulpit Commentary—Genesis*, ed. H.D.M. Spence and Joseph S. Exell (Grand Rapids, MI: Eerdmans).

Wigram, George W. (1890), *The Englishman's Hebrew and Chaldee Concordance of the Old Testament* (Grand Rapids, MI: Baker, 1980 reprint).

Williams, George (1960), *The Student's Commentary on the Holy Scriptures* (Grand Rapids, MI: Kregel), sixth edition.

Witherspoon, John (1815), *The Works of John Witherspoon* (Edinburgh: J. Ogle).

Wright, Wendy (2003), "Citizens Organize Events to Support Chief Justice Moore," [On-line], URL: http://www.cwfa.org/articles/4428/CWA/freedom/index.htm.